# The Environmental Movement

# The Environmental Movement

From Its Roots to the Challenges of a New Century

## Laurence Pringle

HarperCollins*Publishers*

Permission to use the following photographs is gratefully acknowledged: AP Photo/Jeff Barnard, pp. 98–99; Bureau of Land Management, p. 34; Electrical Power Research Institute, pp. 65, 78; Exxon, p. 124; John Goodwin, pp. 11, 85, 89; Magnum Photos, Inc., © 1962 by Erich Hartmann, p. 45; The Metropolitan Museum of Art, gift in memory of Jonathan Sturges by his children, 1895, p. 19; Michigan Conservation Department, p. 47; National Aeronautics and Space Administration (NASA), p. 54; National Oceanic and Atmospheric Administration (NOAA), p. 81; National Park Service, pp. 28, 32–33, 115; National Science Foundation, p. 74; The Nature Conservancy, pp. 8, 96; United Nations, p. 111; University of Wisconsin-Madison Archives, p. 38; USDA Photo/J. Clark, p. 41; U.S. Fish and Wildlife Service, p. 122; Mr. and Mrs. W. D. Weiss, Buffalo Bill Historical Center, p. 15. All other photographs by the author. Paintings on pp. 13, 21, 24–25 reproduced from the collections of the Library of Congress. Cartoon on p. 69: Dan Wasserman © 1983 *Los Angeles Times*. Reprinted with permission. Cartoon on p. 95: reprinted with permission of Joe Heller, *Green Bay Press-Gazette.*

The Environmental Movement
Copyright © 2000 by Laurence Pringle

Library of Congress Cataloging-in-Publication Data
Pringle, Laurence P.
The environmental movement: from its roots to the challenges of a new century / Laurence Pringle.
p. cm.
Includes bibliographical references and index.
Summary: Chronicles the history, key players, and future challenges of the environmental movement.
ISBN 0-688-15626-6
1.Environmentalism—History Juvenile literature. [1. Environmental protection. 2. Environmentalists.]
I. Title. GE195.5.P76 2000 363.7'0525'09—dc21 99-32110 CIP

10 9 8 7 6 5 4 3 2 1
❖
First Edition

*For James K. "Jake" Page, a fine writer
and a good friend, with fond memories of gatherings
at Macomb Street.*

# Contents

# Introduction

To some, *environmentalist* is a dirty word. Environmentalists have been called prophets of doom, tree huggers, and job killers. Some business spokespersons and conservative commentators believe that the "Red menace" of communism has been replaced by the "Green menace" of environmentalism.

In the eyes of the general public, however, the environmental movement is a respected and noble cause. Opinion polls conducted in the 1990s found that 81 percent of adult Americans said they were either "active environmentalists" or "sympathetic toward environmental concerns."

Nevertheless, the environmental movement will always have opponents and critics. It promotes change—in ways of thinking as well as in ways of acting. It was probably the most powerful social revolution of the twentieth century. Environmentalism has affected our legal system, educational system, economy, and politics. It has affected the design and construction of buildings and automobiles and many other aspects of day-to-day life. It will continue to promote and cause change in the twenty-first century.

This book digs into history to uncover the roots of this extraordinary force and then describes key events during several stages, or "waves," of progress in the last thirty years of the twentieth century. It tells how small numbers of writers, thinkers, scientists, and politicians have played large roles in the environmental movement and how today many others also help—locally, nationally, and globally.

Finally, this book confronts a new century and describes some of the trends and challenges that lie ahead for the environmental movement.

FOUR OUT OF FIVE PEOPLE IN THE UNITED STATES SUPPORT ENVIRONMENTAL CAUSES. LIKE THIS FAMILY IN TEXAS THAT VOLUNTEERED TO PLANT NATIVE SPECIES, SOME TAKE ACTION.

# 1
# Roots

(FIFTEENTH—MID-NINETEENTH
CENTURY)

Be fertile and increase,
fill the earth and subdue
it and have dominion
over the fish of the sea
and over the fowl of
the air and over every
living thing that creepeth
upon the earth.

—The Bible, Genesis 1:28

We have dominated the
earth and subdued
the fish of the sea,
and the results are
terrifying.

—Rabbi James Prosnit
*Amicus Journal* (Winter 1990)

## HOUSEHOLD WORDS

Earth Day, observed each April, is dedicated to the environment on which we all depend. It is a day of celebration, education, and protest.

The first Earth Day, held on April 22, 1970, marked a turning point in the history of public understanding of nature and of humankind's place in it. During the months leading up to the first Earth Day and for months afterward, news media focused on pollution and other harm done to the air, water, and land. Millions of people were introduced to the word *environment*.

The environment is the total of all conditions that surround and affect a living thing. It includes the air, water, land, and living things. By 1970 most people in the United States, Canada, and many other nations had begun to recognize that a polluted environment can threaten more than the survival of birds or fish. It can threaten humans too.

For the first time millions of people were also introduced to the word *ecology*. This is a science, the study of the relationships between living things and their environments. Compared with physics and astronomy, ecology is a fairly young science (it was first defined in 1866). However, it is vitally important and is a key to understanding our environment.

Since 1970 these terms—*environment* and *ecology*—have become household words. People who are active in reducing pollution, protecting threatened wildlife habitats, and confronting similar issues are called environmentalists.

PARADES, DEMONSTRATIONS, AND OTHER GATHERINGS HIGHLIGHTED THE FIRST EARTH DAY AND HELPED FOCUS PUBLIC ATTENTION ON THE ENVIRONMENT.

Their collective effort is a social and political force called the environmental movement. Since 1970 this movement has caused change and sparked controversy, not just in North America but all over the world. It will continue to do so as people face environmental problems and choices in the new century.

Before we consider what lies ahead for the environmental movement, however, it is important to explore its beginnings. The values that environmentalists express today can be traced back centuries.

## NATURE'S MASTERS OR PARTNERS?

To many of the Europeans who came to North America, the New World was a frightening place of vast, dark forests, predatory beasts, and "savage" natives. In September 1620 Pilgrim leader William Bradford observed what is now Cape Cod, Massachusetts, from the deck of the *Mayflower* and wrote of "a hideous and desolate wilderness full of wilde beasts and wilde men."

Clearly—to Bradford—North America needed to be tamed, its wildness subdued. He and other Europeans had their own idea of what a proper landscape looked like: a garden. This view is still with us and to a certain extent explains why some people from the eastern United States expect to have grassy lawns when they relocate to the deserts of the Southwest.

To the European explorers the New World was also a vast treasury of wealth: gold, timber, fertile soils, fish and wildlife, and other resources. Explorers reported wildlife and fish in incredible and "inexhaustible" abundance. When the supplies of wildlife dwindled and forests were cut in one place, it seemed there were always more to the west. The natural environment of North America changed rapidly as people cleared forests, plowed fields, drained swamps, built roads and houses, and killed wildlife for food or to protect livestock.

TO EUROPEAN COLONISTS NORTH AMERICA SEEMED TO HAVE AN INEXHAUSTIBLE ABUNDANCE OF NATURAL RESOURCES.

Colonists and settlers encountered the people who had originally settled North America. The Indians, as they were mistakenly called, had ideas about the land and its life that contrasted sharply with those of the invading Europeans. They saw themselves as part of the natural world—nature's partners. Europeans saw themselves as separate and above the natural world—nature's masters.

The Indians were puzzled by the white settlers' apparent contempt for the earth and by the notion that a person could "own" a piece of land, a length of a river, or part of a lakeshore. Separate tribes went to war over territories, but no individual Indian thought of owning land. In contrast, one of the first goals of settlers from Europe was to claim ownership of land. This led to many misunderstandings, and to broken treaties, with the Indians.

In 1877 Chief Joseph was asked to surrender Nez Percé land to white settlers. He protested that he had no right to do so. He said, "The one who has the right to dispose of it is the one who has created it." He added, "We are contented to let things remain as the Great Spirit made them. The white men are not, and will change the rivers and mountains if they do not suit them." (Ironically, as former Secretary of the Interior Stewart Udall wrote in his 1963 book *The Quiet Crisis,* today we find ourselves "turning back to the ancient Indian land ideas, to the Indian understanding that we are not outside of nature, but of it.")

Native Americans have been called the first environmentalists. Historians give us evidence that they were appalled by the wastefulness of Europeans—for example, by shooting bison and taking only their tongues, which were considered a delicacy. Plains Indians used almost all of a slain bison. There is also evidence that Native Americans observed nature and wisely applied their knowledge. For instance, they deliberately set fires in some habitats to release natural fertilizers that spurred plant growth and to increase wildlife populations.

Still, it would be a mistake to conclude that the first Americans lived in

---

THE NATIVE AMERICANS OBSERVED THAT PRAIRIE FIRES WERE A BENEFIT FOR PLANTS AND WILDLIFE, AND SOMETIMES SET FIRES DELIBERATELY.

...y with the land. Archaeologists have discovered that the Anasazi people who flourished in New Mexico's Chaco Canyon from about A.D. 1000 to 1200 had to abandon the area because they had destroyed its resources. They had used up the local woodlands for fuel and building. Erosion had carried away the topsoil of their farms and ruined water channels that had been vital for carrying irrigation water.

However, overall Indians had little impact on nature because their numbers were few. In 1492, when Christopher Columbus reached the island of San Salvador, only an estimated four million people lived in North America. Would a much greater population of Native Americans, with better weapons and tools, have used North American resources more wisely than the Europeans? Because their lands were taken from them, we shall never know. We do know, though, that Indians were drawn into the market economy of the Europeans. They traded food and furs for blankets, axes, guns, and other goods. For the first time the resources of North America were exported to European countries. When hats made of beaver fur became fashionable abroad, Native Americans helped destroy beaver populations in eastern Canada and New England.

Even though Indians had a sense of being connected to nature in a way that was not understood by most Europeans, the roots of the environmental movement cannot be traced to Native Americans any more than they can to the settlers and ordinary citizens who were busy subduing a continent. So where did the concept of environmentalism originate?

## THE SOURCES OF ENVIRONMENTALISM

The ideas behind what we now call environmentalism stem from several sources. They came from a few educated travelers who had seen abused land and polluted waters in Europe. Beginning in the mid-eighteenth century, these travelers warned that the incredible beauty and "unlimited" bounty of resources in the New World were vanishing. Ideas also came from a few leaders in eastern North America, where timber, wildlife, and other resources were exploited first and where the damage to the land and waters was most clear. Records of New England town meetings in the seventeenth century show that voices were raised against the ruthless destruction of forests and overgrazing by cattle.

In addition, some early presidents of the United States expressed concern about environmental damage. Thomas Jefferson, president from 1801 to 1809, attempted to halt soil erosion on the fields of his Virginia estate. James Madison, whose administration ran from 1809 to 1817, also voiced his concern about soil erosion: "With . . . so little attention paid to the means of repairing the ravages, no one can be surprised at the impoverished face of the country."

While soil erosion hurts farmers directly because it can reduce crop yields and thereby decrease their income, concern about it does not get to the heart of environmental awareness, which calls for respect for all of nature, not just for those resources that have dollar value. This deeper level of concern came from writers, philosophers, scientists, scholars, ministers, and others, including painters of North America's landscapes and wildlife. As a result, in both North America and Europe the 1800s brought an increased appreciation of the beauty of nature, especially of untouched wilderness.

In the 1830s George Catlin made paintings of Native Americans and the wildlife of the Great Plains. He was the first to call for a huge "nation's park." In a journal he kept during his travels he wrote: "What a beautiful and thrilling specimen for America to preserve and hold up to the view of her refined citizens and the world, in future ages!" (Almost forty years were to pass before the first national park was created in North America.)

Some writers and philosophers of that time adhered to a philosophy called romanticism. They held a romantic view of nature, believing that people were happier when they were close to nature. Some writers, including Ralph Waldo Emerson, believed that appreciating nature would lead inevitably to a belief in God. For all humans, he wrote, "The first in time and the first in importance of the influences on the mind is that of Nature."

The works of a group of artists known as the Hudson River school showed wild landscapes at their best. The message of the art was: This is not something to subdue; this is something to inspire you, to cherish, to preserve.

Henry David Thoreau was a pupil of Emerson's. His writings, especially *Walden* (published in 1854), warned of the threats to nature and, therefore, to humans, from the rapid advance of industrialism. He offered few solutions since he had little faith in the workings of government. However, he raised basic questions about how life ought to be lived and about what gives meaning to life. He celebrated wild nature: "In wildness is the preservation of the world." More than a century and a half later these words continue to inspire people to fight for the preservation of wild places.

Some of Thoreau's actions and words foreshadowed developments in the environmental movement. In 1845 he was briefly jailed because he refused to pay federal taxes that could be used to finance the United States' war with Mexico. This was "civil disobedience" (the title of Thoreau's 1849 essay). More than a century later peaceful protests were important weapons in both the environmental and civil rights movements.

While Thoreau rarely left his home in Concord, Massachusetts, another writer, born in Vermont in 1801, traveled widely and brought a global perspective to his observations about humans and nature. He was George Perkins Marsh. Of all those who nurtured the roots of the environmental movement,

THE GLORY OF WILD LANDSCAPES WAS CAPTURED BY PAINTERS OF THE HUDSON RIVER
SCHOOL. THIS IS *VIEW OF THE CATSKILL, EARLY AUTUMN*, BY THOMAS COLE.

Marsh is considered the most important influence in the nineteenth century.

He was bright, curious, and ambitious. In Vermont he was a naturalist, teacher, and lawyer. He operated a rock quarry and a woolens mill and also edited a newspaper. He was elected to Congress and later served as ambassador first to Turkey and then to Italy. In Europe, the Near East, and North America he observed the land, waters, and wildlife. While abroad, he saw man-made deserts and the ruins of past civilizations. He envisioned a similar disaster looming ahead in North America. Loggers had stripped New England of forests and were in the process of deforesting the Midwest. Within sixty years they had cleared an area the size of Europe of forests.

Marsh learned to read in twenty languages in order to gain as much knowledge as possible about what we now call the environment. He summed up his observations and findings in a book: *Man and Nature; or, Physical Geography as Modified by Human Action.* Until its publication in 1864 most people believed that nature could quickly heal damage caused by humans. However, from what he had seen in areas of Asia and Africa, and in Greece and other parts of Europe, Marsh was led to believe that "man has brought the face of the earth to a desolation almost as complete as that of the moon." He wrote: "Man is everywhere a disturbing agent. Wherever he plants his foot, the harmonies of nature are turned to discord."

Though the word *ecology* had not yet been coined, *Man and Nature* included ecological observations. For example, Marsh noticed that insect pest numbers exploded when their natural enemies were killed. By killing certain insect-eating birds, Marsh wrote, man was "waging a treacherous war on his natural allies."

When he wrote of humans "breaking up the floor and wainscoting and doors and window frames of our dwelling," the dwelling to which he referred was the earth. Another century was to pass before the general public grasped the idea that the earth is a vulnerable home.

George Perkins Marsh sensed, correctly, that humans would make more powerful machines and invent new technology with which to change and harm "our dwelling," the earth. However, he was a hopeful man. He urged intense study of the human impact on nature before it was too late. With knowledge and action, he wrote, the harm to our dwelling place could be halted and even repaired.

GEORGE PERKINS MARSH WAS REMARKABLY WELL EDUCATED AND WELL TRAVELED. HE
WARNED AMERICANS THAT DESTRUCTION OF THEIR OWN MAKING MIGHT LIE AHEAD.

# 2

## The Rise of Conservation

(MID-NINETEENTH–MID-TWENTIETH CENTURY)

We abuse land because we regard it as commodity belonging to us. When we see land as a community to which we belong, we may begin to use it with love and respect.

—Aldo Leopold, *A Sand County Almanac* (1949)

## CONSERVATION AND THE FEDERAL GOVERNMENT

*Man and Nature* had no immediate effect in the United States. In 1872, a few years after the book's publication, the U.S. Congress passed a law that allowed anyone to stake a mining claim on public land, even on parkland. Most politicians then believed that unbridled development was good for the nation. This law, which was still in force in 1999, was just one of many government giveaways of public resources to private interests.

Many attempts to halt the misuse of resources were defeated. Carl Schurz, U.S. secretary of the interior in 1877, tried to establish careful management of forests on public lands and to punish people who cut illegally from publicly owned forests. But the timber barons, as they were called, persuaded Congress to undermine this attempt at reform. Years later, in 1889, Schurz described the disappointing experience:

*I observed enterprising timber thieves not merely stealing trees, but stealing whole forests. I observed hundreds of sawmills in full blast, devoted exclusively to the sawing up of timber from public lands. . . . The recommendations of rational forest planning went for nothing. Some laws were indeed passed but they appeared rather to favor the taking of timber from the public land rather than to stop it. . . . Deaf was Congress and deaf the people seemed to be.*

On other issues, however, some people were not deaf to cries of alarm about damage to the environment. They prodded the city, state, and federal governments to take action. Citizen groups caused the first city air pollution laws to be passed, in an attempt to reduce the smoke and soot from wood- and coal-burning furnaces. Some parks and wild places were set aside for the enjoyment of later generations. In 1872, 2 million acres located mostly in northwestern Wyoming were protected as Yellowstone National Park. In the last decade of the nineteenth century the United States also began to establish a system of forest reserves. By 1897 these reserves totaled 34 million acres. They were the foundation for the national forests, which now include 160 million acres, mostly in the western United States.

## THE INFLUENCE OF EARLY ACTIVISTS

When the government did take steps to protect resources, it was often in response to the efforts of one person, or a small group, trying to influence lawmaking. One such person was John Muir, born in 1838, who loved mountainous wilderness, especially California's Sierra Nevada and Yosemite Valley. He expressed his appreciation of unspoiled nature in articles that were published in nationally circulated magazines and read by many people. In 1892 he became

the first president of a new group committed to preserving wilderness, the Sierra Club. It had three main goals: to explore, enjoy, and protect wild places.

Another concerned citizen was George Bird Grinnell, born in 1849, a wealthy New Yorker who was fascinated by nature. He published a magazine, *Forest and Stream,* whose readers were hunters and others interested in the outdoors. In the magazine Grinnell wrote about the devastating loss of wildlife across North America. He tried to establish a group dedicated to protecting birds. Founded in 1886, it was named the Audubon Society, after the great bird artist John James Audubon.

This national group failed, for lack of money, though local and state Audubon groups continued, grew,

HUNTERS AND OTHER OUTDOORSMEN WERE AMONG THE EARLY LEADERS OF THE CONSERVATION MOVEMENT. THEY ADVOCATED SUCH RESTRICTIONS AS LIMITING THE NUMBER OF ANIMALS TAKEN IN ORDER TO HALT WASTEFUL SLAUGHTER, LIKE THIS SCENE IN TEXAS.

and eventually formed the National Audubon Society in 1905. Meanwhile, in 1887 Grinnell and others had formed another group, called the Boone and Crockett Club (it was named for pioneers Daniel Boone and Davy Crockett). Nearly all club members were hunters and outdoorsmen who were appalled at the slaughter of wildlife across North America. Many mammals and birds were being killed by "goon" hunters, then discarded without being used for food. Others were killed by commercial hunters for sale. The Boone and Crockett Club promoted ethical standards for hunting. It advocated laws that would allow wildlife populations to recover, for example, by limiting the number of animals taken and not allowing hunting when animals were raising their young.

At the turn of the century most of the citizens who were actively fighting for the protection of wildlife and other resources were educated, wealthy men who hunted, fished, hiked, and camped. To some extent their efforts were selfish: They wanted fish to catch and wild turkeys, ducks, deer, and other wildlife to hunt. However, they also wanted everyone, including future generations, to be able to experience wild lands, wildlife, and unpolluted waters. Since these men had some wealth, they were able to travel and see firsthand how resources were being abused all over North America.

## THE CONSERVATION PRESIDENT

Theodore Roosevelt was one such man. A founding member of the Boone and Crockett Club, he was deeply concerned about the loss of forests, wildlife, and other resources. Early in the twentieth century Teddy Roosevelt became president of the United States. He served from 1901 to 1909. Protecting nature and its resources was a major goal of his administration, and no president who followed in the twentieth century accomplished as much as TR, as he was sometimes called.

Roosevelt camped in the Sierra Nevada with John Muir and shared his love of wilderness. However, TR's chief adviser on natural resources was Gifford Pinchot, a Pennsylvanian who had studied forestry in Europe. Although forestry as a profession was practically unknown in North America, in Germany and some other northern European countries, people had begun to manage forests with the best scientific knowledge then available. This was the sort of expertise that Pinchot had brought back to the United States. He had become a friend and adviser of Theodore Roosevelt's when TR was governor of New York. During Roosevelt's administration Pinchot was put in charge of the new U.S. Forest Service.

Pinchot had a name for his approach to protecting resources and using them wisely. He called it conservation. (Pinchot did not actually coin the word; George Perkins Marsh had used it in his book *Man and Nature.*) Pinchot realized that conservation based on scientific knowledge was needed for all resources, not just forests.

Pinchot promoted this idea in his speeches and writings, including a 1910 book, *The Fight for Conservation.* In it he wrote: "Conservation is the most democratic movement this country has known for a generation. It holds that people have not only the right, but the duty to control the use of natural resources. . . . Conservation is the application of commonsense to the common problems for the common good."

As a hunter and camper with a lifelong passion for nature, Theodore Roosevelt was fertile soil for the seeds of conservation. He became "the conservation president," much to the consternation of those who were growing rich by exploiting resources without any thought of later generations.

Roosevelt brought many millions of acres under the protection of the U.S. Forest Service, which was responsible for managing woodlands and other

resources wisely. Beginning with Pelican Island in Florida, he established fifty federal wildlife refuges across the nation. He urged passage of the Antiquities Act of 1906. While this law was mainly aimed at protecting archaeological sites from thieves, TR used it broadly to protect a variety of threatened sites. Once set aside, they were called national monuments. For example, Grand Canyon National Monument was established in 1908. Later in the century many of these protected areas, including Grand Canyon, became national parks. About a quarter of all U.S. national parks owe their original protection to the Antiquities Act—and to Roosevelt's creative use of it.

In 1908 TR called all state governors to a White House Conference on Conservation. The emphasis of this meeting was the preservation of forests, wildlife, and similar resources, but the protection of human health was also cited as a goal of conservation. Inclusion of the human condition broadened the definition of *conservation* as well as support for the conservation movement, the forerunner of the environmental movement.

## CONSERVATION AND PRESERVATION

Conservation efforts were opposed by timber and mining companies and other industries. Sometimes the idea of conservation of some areas was also opposed by John Muir and others who treasured wilderness. Their goal was the *preservation* of wild places, keeping them wild, not the judicious extraction of timber, minerals, and other resources.

This difference in attitudes still exists. It sometimes leads to conflict between environmental groups that are usually allies. This tension can also be

IN MAY 1903 THEODORE ROOSEVELT AND JOHN MUIR CAMPED NEAR GLACIER POINT ABOVE THE YOSEMITE VALLEY. THESE TWO CONSERVATIONISTS AGREED ON THE NEED TO SET ASIDE WILD AREAS ACROSS THE NATION.

found within the government agencies that oversee natural resources. Early in the twentieth century it led to conflict between Gifford Pinchot and John Muir.

Pinchot emphasized the wise use aspect of conservation. His goal was to guard and manage resources so their economic benefits would continue over time. Muir, on the other hand, believed that some places in nature were too precious to be exploited for their resources, such as timber, that had dollar value. He believed that humans are part of nature and have no special rights to change and destroy the living places of other forms of life. If there ever were a war between humans and the wild beasts, Muir said, "I would be tempted to sympathize with the bears."

President Roosevelt tended to agree with Pinchot. Muir was not invited to the 1908 White House Conference on Conservation.

The conflict between conservation and preservation led to a major battle that involved the whole nation. With debates in Congress, editorials in newspapers, and articles in magazines, it was a preview of many environmental battles to come.

The issue was the fate of a wild valley in California's Sierra Nevada. Hetch Hetchy Valley lay within the borders of Yosemite National Park. In beauty many considered it a twin of the spectacular Yosemite Valley. However, Hetch Hetchy's characteristics—steep rock walls, a narrow outlet—also made it an ideal site for a dam and reservoir that would supply some of San Francisco's growing need for drinking water.

Pinchot favored the damming of the valley. Muir, the Sierra Club, and other wilderness advocates opposed it. Since the valley was within a national park, editorials in many newspapers chose the preservation side of the argument. President Roosevelt was indecisive but eventually supported Pinchot. Several years after Roosevelt left office, during the administration of President Woodrow Wilson, Congress approved the Hetch Hetchy Dam, and the valley was flooded.

# THE GROWTH OF CONSERVATION GROUPS

Muir died in 1914, and with him died some of the spark of those who fought for wilderness. Roosevelt was followed by presidents who cared little about conservation. Some tried to undo his accomplishments. Part of the reason for this lack of concern may have been the times themselves. The entire nation was distracted by World War I (1914–1918), which the U.S. entered in 1917, and then by a deep economic depression during the 1930s. For many people, concern about conservation seemed to be an unaffordable luxury.

Nevertheless, the conservation movement grew. Local groups sprang up. New national groups formed. One, the General Wildlife Federation, organized in 1937, was inspired by J. N. ("Ding") Darling, the head of the Bureau of Biological Survey, a wildlife research agency of the federal government (now the Fish and Wildlife Service). He was responsible for passage of a law that requires duck and goose hunters to buy annual federal duck stamps. Money from sales of these stamps has provided the national government with many millions of dollars that are used for acquiring national wildlife refuges.

Darling learned that there were more than thirty-five thousand local and state groups in the United States that could be loosely called conservation organizations. Many were made up of hunters or fishermen; others were devoted to nature study or protecting wild places. Darling urged that they join together, become more politically active, and work toward common goals. This "federation" of sportsmen's clubs and other groups became the General Wildlife Federation. In 1938 its name was changed to the National Wildlife Federation. Its first political success was to convince Congress to establish a tax on firearms, with the funds being used to support wildlife conservation efforts in every state.

During the early decades of the twentieth century, the most blatant slaughter of wildlife, timber thievery, and other illegal abuses of natural

resources were halted. However, both conservation and preservation groups had to fight battle after battle. Ironically, many of the conflicts involved agencies of the government that had been set up to safeguard and to manage resources. These agencies, including the National Park Service, the Forest Service, and the Fish and Wildlife Service, were tugged in different directions by opposing forces. The Forest Service, for instance, manages all the national forests and the multiple uses to which they can be put. These uses may include growing timber, allowing livestock to graze, providing habitat for fish and wildlife, and facilitating recreation, including camping, hiking, fishing, and hunting. Throughout most of the twentieth century, the uses with ready dollar values—timber cutting and grazing—have been emphasized. These have

THE FATE OF THE HETCH HETCHY VALLEY BECAME A NATIONAL ISSUE IN THE EARLY 1900s. EVENTUALLY MOST OF ITS WILD BEAUTY WAS FLOODED BY A RESERVOIR.

often hurt the other uses of national forests. For example, logging has often been allowed close to streams, with debris and silt from erosion damaging the habitats of trout, salmon, and other aquatic life.

## ALDO LEOPOLD, A PIONEER ECOLOGIST

In the first half of the twentieth century government agencies managed forests, wildlife populations, and other resources with limited knowledge because no one had a good understanding of how nature "worked." As a result, they sometimes did more harm than good. A few individuals began to question the wisdom of these conservation efforts. One such person was Aldo Leopold. Once a forester who eagerly carried out the policies of the U.S. Forest Service, Leopold observed the results, changed his ideas, and wrote eloquently about the need for a new relationship with nature.

A collection of his essays, *A Sand County Almanac,* was first published in 1949. A person reading it today might think, "Yes, that's true—I learned that in school." In mid-century, however, Leopold's writings were revolutionary. Today *A Sand County Almanac* is considered one of the most important books published in the twentieth century. Of it, historian and conservationist Wallace Stegner wrote in 1990: "It is a superb distillation of what many Americans had been groping toward for more than a century."

Born in 1887, Aldo Leopold grew up along the Mississippi River in Iowa. He studied forestry at Yale University and learned Gifford Pinchot's ideas about forest management. He became supervisor of the Carson National Forest in New Mexico in 1913. His work included having roads built for

LIVESTOCK GRAZING, LOGGING, AND MINING ARE ALLOWED ON MANY KINDS OF PUBLIC LANDS. THEY CAN HARM SOILS, STREAMS, AND WILDLIFE.

loggers and fighting forest fires. More interested in wildlife than in forestry, he was a naturalist and a hunter. For a time he accepted the idea that there were "useful" animals—those that could be hunted or fished—and that their numbers could be increased if wolves, bobcats, and other predators were killed. In 1920 Leopold wrote: "It is going to take patience and money to catch the last wolf or mountain lion in New Mexico, but the last one must be caught before the job can be called fully successful."

Leopold held several positions in the Forest Service in the Southwest. In 1933 he became professor of game management at the University of Wisconsin. By then his teaching, writing, and speeches were challenging some attitudes held by many conservationists and by the general public. His words were backed by evidence from the Southwest and elsewhere. For example, reports from Arizona suggested that an all-out war on wolves and other large predators in the Grand Canyon area had backfired. The deer population rose dramatically. The animals stripped the land bare of edible plants; then many starved to death.

The more Leopold learned about nature, the more he questioned the kind of conservation then being practiced. He visited the heavily managed tree farm forests of Germany that had inspired Gifford Pinchot and found them sadly lacking in a variety of plant and animal life. Predators had been killed there too, and deer were in poor health. Leopold began to see that predators played an important role in the overall health of the land.

He also saw the wisdom of setting aside unspoiled wild areas, for both their aesthetic value and their value for scientific research. While with the Forest Service, he had drafted the plan for preserving part of the Gila National Forest as the nation's first wilderness area. In 1935 Leopold became a founding member of the Wilderness Society, which began to fight for lands to be designated as true wilderness, not open to road building and recreational development as

ONCE AN ADVOCATE OF KILLING WOLVES AND OTHER PREDATORS, ALDO LEOPOLD LEARNED OF THE VITAL ROLE THEY PLAY IN NATURE.

national parks and national forests were. (The Wilderness Society led the effort to influence Congress to establish a national system of roadless primitive areas. This was accomplished with the Wilderness Act of 1964.)

In 1938 Leopold changed the name of the university course he taught to Wildlife Ecology. The term *ecology* had been coined in 1866 by the German

biologist Ernst Haeckel. It comes from two Greek words, *oikos,* which means "house" or "place to live," and *logos,* which means "study." Thus, ecology is the study of the houses, or environments, of living things, of all their surroundings, including other organisms, climate, soils, and so on. Ecology is the one science that uses information from almost all other sciences.

Aldo Leopold drew upon his own experience, his research, and the studies of others to begin to change the entire conservation movement. Some of his ideas were not entirely new. He had a complete set of Thoreau's works and was obviously inspired by this philosopher.

Leopold wrote graceful, clear, powerful prose, and his words continue to influence people today. As biologist Victor Scheffer wrote in his 1991 book *The Shaping of Environmentalism in America,* "What Bach gave to music, Leopold gave to environmentalism: its basic vocabulary."

Leopold introduced readers to a new way of thinking about the earth. In the last essay in *A Sand County Almanac* he calls for a new land ethic, a guide for judging the wisdom of human actions: "A thing is right when it tends to pre-serve the integrity, stability, and beauty of the biotic community. It is wrong when it tends otherwise." He explained that the land ethic "enlarges the boundaries of the community, to include soils, waters, plants, and animals, or collectively: the land." A true land ethic, he concluded, "changes the role of *Homo sapiens* from conqueror of the land community to plain member and citizen of it."

Aldo Leopold's greatest contribution was not expressing strong feelings about the wonders of nature or the joys to be found in wilderness. Muir, Thoreau, and others had done that. Rather, as Wallace Stegner pointed out in his writings about Leopold, "he brought as much sensitivity as Thoreau to his study of nature, and more science."

Leopold introduced readers to such ideas and terms as *ecology, biotic community, food chain,* and *ecosystem.* He saw that there were sound *scientific* reasons for caring about and protecting nature and wild habitats. The decades since his death, in 1948, have only confirmed the keenness of his vision.

# 3
# New Concerns, New Strength
## (1945–1970)

We still talk in terms of conquest. We still haven't become mature enough to think of ourselves as only a very tiny part of a vast and incredible universe. . . . We're challenged, as mankind has never been challenged before, to prove our maturity and our mastery, not of nature but of ourselves.

—Rachel Carson, *Silent Spring* (1962)

## ENVIROMENTAL ISSUES HIT HOME

After World War II ended in 1945, the United States entered the second half of the twentieth century in an upbeat mood. Inexpensive automobiles and gasoline allowed people to drive to work. Plastics, new kinds of fertilizers, long-lasting insecticides, and other innovative products seemed to promise a better, easier life. It was a time of hubris—extreme, unjustified confidence.

As George Perkins Marsh had warned nearly a century before, humans had invented powerful new tools that would pose great threats to nature, but the threats were not recognized right away. During most of the 1950s conservationists focused on familiar issues: the protection of fish, wildlife, and wild places. They opposed the dam-building agenda of the U.S. Army Corps of Engineers.

They urged government agencies to take better care of the resources they administered. One such agency was the Bureau of Land Management (BLM), which oversees the use of 246 million acres of land in the West. Conservationists jokingly referred to the BLM as the Bureau of Livestock and Mining.

INEXPENSIVE CARS AND GASOLINE MADE IT POSSIBLE FOR SUBURBS TO SPRAWL OUTWARD FROM CITIES. IN THE PROCESS THEY TOOK OVER MILLIONS OF ACRES OF FARMLAND.

A SIGN WARNS OF POLLUTED WATER. OCCURRENCES LIKE THIS ALL OVER THE NATION CON-
TRIBUTED TO A GROWING CONCERN ABOUT THE ENVIRONMENT.

The conservation movement was changing, however. From its beginnings until the 1950s it owed most of its strength and success to hunters, fishermen, and nature lovers. Then, thanks partly to Aldo Leopold, scientists increasingly became more involved in conservation issues. At first they were mostly scientists who studied living things—ecologists, botanists, ornithologists. Later, scientists in such fields as medicine, public health, and the chemistry of the atmosphere supported the movement.

Often it was not a case of a scientist's claiming a wealth of information on an issue. One ecologist said of the world's ecosystem, "It is not only more complex than we think. It is more complex than we *can* think." Since nature was so poorly understood, some scientists cautioned, humans would be wise to treat it with care and respect. As the link between conservation and science grew stronger, the conservation movement gained credibility in legislative chambers and courtrooms and in the eyes of the public.

By the early 1960s many people were becoming concerned about the quality of their everyday life. They commuted to work in choking polluted air. They found beaches littered with garbage, or massive fish kills, or tar balls from oil spills. They worried about possible threats they could not see—for instance, radiation drifting down from the sky from aboveground tests of nuclear weapons. While many conservation issues may have seemed remote and irrelevant, now people worried about their own health, the health of their children, and the health of generations to come.

## RACHEL CARSON, SILENT SPRING, AND DDT

In 1962 a book was published that brought a general worry about health threats from the environment into focus on one issue. It became a best-seller, stirred great interest, and loosed a flood of sharp criticism. The book was

*Silent Spring.* The author was Rachel Carson.

As a college student Carson agonized over a career choice: to be a scientist or a writer? A biology professor convinced her she could be both. After graduation she earned a master's degree, then began study for a doctorate in zoology. She had to drop out for lack of money. (Not having a Ph.D. hurt her later, when critics accused her of being an amateur scientist.) In 1936 Carson was hired as an aquatic biologist by a federal agency that later became part of the Fish and Wildlife Service.

Rachel Carson had a burning curiosity and a gift for poetic writing. Learning more and more about marine life, she began to write magazine articles about the sea. Her first book, *Under the Sea Wind,* was published in 1941. Her second, *The Sea Around Us* (1951), won a National Book Award. Carson had rare talent. As her biographer Paul Brooks explained, "The merging of these two powerful currents—the imagination and insight of a creative writer with a scientist's passion for fact—goes far to explain the blend of beauty and authority that was to make her books unique."

Her writing success allowed her to stop working for the government. However, she kept in touch with biologists at the Fish and Wildlife Service. From them she learned of the dangers to birds and other forms of life from new kinds of insecticides. When a friend in Massachusetts told of birds dropping dead after an area had been sprayed to kill mosquitoes, Rachel Carson gathered more information about insecticides. Four years of research and writing led to *Silent Spring.*

Before the book was published, parts of it appeared in the *New Yorker* magazine. A fierce backlash from the chemical industry began, and an effort was made to stop publication of the book. Before *Silent Spring* was published, and for many months after, it was severely criticized by "experts," some of whom had not even read it.

Part of this fierce opposition was understandable because *Silent Spring* warned of the harm being done by long-lasting insecticides, especially DDT. This poison was seen as a chemical hero by many. Its Swiss inventor, Paul Müller, had won the 1948 Nobel Prize for physiology or medicine. Health officials credited DDT with saving millions of lives by halting typhus and malaria epidemics in Europe. Farmers and foresters hailed DDT's effectiveness, as did backyard gardeners. The fact that DDT did not break down easily, remaining poisonous for many years, seemed to be a virtue to many people.

*Silent Spring* revealed the dark side of DDT. Carson reported evidence that biologists had found: DDT was passing through food chains, harming fish and wildlife

IN HER BOOK *SILENT SPRING* RACHEL CARSON WARNED OF THE EFFECTS OF LONG-LASTING PESTICIDES AS THEY MOVED THROUGH FOOD CHAINS.

and even reaching humans. Moreover, the scientists warned, insect pests were developing resistance to DDT, as they had to pesticides before (houseflies in Italy and the United States had evolved resistance to DDT by 1948).

Carson acknowledged that pesticides had done good work in combating pests. But she was very concerned about the bad effects that were being ignored. As a biologist and ecologist, she believed there was something terribly wrong about spraying thousands of tons of poisons over the earth with so little knowledge of their effects. She pointed out that these poisons were misnamed. They were not just pesticides—"pest killers." They killed honeybees and other beneficial insects; they killed fish, birds, and many other kinds of animals. They were biocides—"life killers."

Opposition to *Silent Spring* came from four groups that had special interest in continuing the use of pesticides. They were the pesticide industry, officials and scientists working for the U.S. Department of Agriculture, officials and scientists working at agricultural colleges, and medical and public health officials. In book reviews, articles, and public announcements they attacked *Silent Spring.*

A reviewer in *Time* magazine called the book "unfair, one-sided," written with "emotion-fanning words." The critic also said that the text was filled with "oversimplification and downright errors." There is some truth in this. Carson had chosen such chapter titles as "Elixirs of Death" and "Rivers of Death." And there were a few factual errors. However, such criticisms missed the point. Carson had consciously used dramatic phrases and chapter titles, but she had also presented scientific evidence clearly and accurately.

One reviewer accused her of trying "to scare the American public out of its wits." Instead she had tried to scare the American public *into* its wits. Many readers learned that the long-term effects of biocides were poorly understood. (Eventually scientists learned that low levels of DDT caused such birds as eagles and pelicans to produce weak, easily broken eggshells, thereby sabotaging their reproduction.) Use of these poisons was like a giant laboratory experiment on

DDT THREATENED THE SURVIVAL OF SUCH PREDATORY BIRDS AS BALD EAGLES BECAUSE IT HARMED THE EGGSHELL-MAKING PROCESS WITHIN FEMALES.

the earth's animal life, including humans. People realized that they were at the end of food chains. As Rachel Carlson indicated in her book, "For the first time in the history of the world, every human being is now subjected to contact with dangerous chemicals from the moment of conception until death."

*Silent Spring* was not entirely negative. Carson offered evidence that much use (actually *over*use) of biocides could be reduced without cutting crop yields. Biological controls, including the natural enemies of insect pests, could be substituted. Today such methods are more common, though many farmers and gardeners still reach for poisons as a first defense against pests. However, partly thanks to Rachel Carson, the biocides now legally available in the United States do not pose the threats to humans that DDT and similar long-lasting chemicals did.

## CONFRONTING NEW ISSUES

Rachel Carson died in 1964. She did not live to witness the banning of DDT in the United States in 1971. Had she lived another decade or two, she would have enjoyed the belated honor and respect afforded her work in *Silent Spring*. She probably would have written further on the subject. If so, she could have pointed out that U.S. companies still make and sell DDT and other banned poisons abroad, particularly to developing nations that have weak environmental protection laws. (Between 1992 and 1994, for example, U.S. companies exported more than 114,600 tons of biocides banned at home.) She could also have found plenty of evidence that some biocides approved for use in the United States still move through food chains and kill millions of birds in the nation each year.

Had *Silent Spring* been published a decade earlier, in the fifties, its message might not have been heard. But the 1960s provided a ready audience for it. The book brought together many of the concerns that conservationists and preservationists shared with people who were more worried about pollution and human health. It marked another step in the evolution of the conservation movement into the environmental movement.

*Silent Spring* also found a receptive audience because the 1960s were a time of social unrest in the United States. The nation was deeply divided over U.S. involvement in the Vietnam War. There were antiwar marches and civil rights and women's movement demonstrations. It was a time to question values and institutions. Another book published in those times, in 1965, criticized the safety and pollution record of U.S. automobile makers, especially General Motors. The book, *Unsafe at Any Speed,* and its author, Ralph Nader, were attacked by the auto industry, but within a year Congress established an agency to oversee and enforce automobile safety standards.

Although auto safety and pollution could be called consumer's rights issues, in some ways environmentalism also involves consumer issues. For example, being able to buy a refrigerator or lightbulb that is energy-efficient affects the environment. Less electricity needed usually means less fuel burned and less air pollution produced.

During the 1960s, membership grew in the Sierra Club and other older conservation groups. New groups were formed to confront new concerns. One was Zero Population Growth, which stressed the connection between human numbers and demands on the earth's resources. One of its founders was Paul Ehrlich, whose 1968 book, *The Population Bomb*, aroused public concern about this connection. Another group, the Union of Concerned Scientists, founded in 1969, was one of several organizations that focused on the nuclear power industry. The scientific expertise of its founders and staff gave it strong credibility as it raised questions about the safety and costliness of nuclear power and criticized its sometimes lax regulation.

The 1960s were a decade of big steps taken to protect resources and public health. In 1963 nearly all nations with nuclear weapons agreed to stop aboveground tests that strewed radioactive particles through the atmosphere. The

1964 Wilderness Preservation Act began the process of saving some extraordinary wild areas. In l968 Congress passed the National Wild and Scenic Rivers Act. Both the wilderness and the wild rivers systems have since had areas added to them. The nation's first law to protect endangered species was passed in 1966. It applied only to "fish and wildlife." The Endangered Species Conservation Act of 1969 extended protection to crustaceans and mollusks. It also provided for two categories of creatures at risk, "threatened" and "endangered." Under this law eight species of whales were listed as endangered. This brought an end to the American whaling industry and gave the United States some credibility in its efforts to persuade other nations to stop or reduce whaling.

None of these steps was easily achieved. Each new law was a result of years of effort by citizen groups that tried to influence, or lobbied, members of Congress.

## CONSERVATIONISTS TAKE TO THE COURTS

While political maneuvering went on in Washington, D.C., and in state capitals, other important steps were taken in courtrooms, for increasingly in the 1960s people turned to the courts in attempts to block a development or to force a government agency to carry out its responsibilities. They had some success, and a new field of environmental law was created.

One of the first favorable court decisions came in New York State. In 1962 Consolidated Edison, the electric utility in New York City, was given permission by the Federal Power Commission to build a pumped-storage electric generating system. The site was on a beautiful stretch of the Hudson River. The plan involved pumping water from the river up through tunnels in Storm King Mountain to a storage reservoir. The water was to be released downward to generate electricity at times of high power demand.

Conservationists opposed this plan for several reasons, including harm to aquatic life in the river and to scenery. They formed the Scenic Hudson Preservation Conference. A utility spokesman called these opponents "bird-watchers, nature fakers, and militant adversaries of progress."

The decision by the power commission was appealed in court. The commission, arguing that the conservationists had no *standing,* asked the judge to dismiss the case. In other words, because the conservationists would not be hurt

CONSERVATIONISTS WON A LANDMARK COURT DECISION IN THE LEGAL BATTLE OVER A PRO-POSED POWER PLANT ON THE HUDSON RIVER.

economically by the power plant, they had no legal right to sue. In 1965 a court of appeals judge sent the case back to the commission with two important rulings. One was that citizen groups do have legal standing to challenge a project even if it does not harm them economically. They could bring suit because of an "esthetic, conservational, and recreational" interest in an area. The second ruling was that agencies such as the power commission had to prepare their own environmental impact statements, documents that estimate the good, bad, or neutral effects of a project on the environment. The agencies also had to consider alternatives, including the alternative of doing nothing. The power plant was not built.

The Scenic Hudson Preservation Conference (now called Scenic Hudson, Inc.) continues to work against environmentally harmful projects in the lower Hudson River valley and for increased public access to the river's shore. The 1965 Storm King ruling on citizens' standing in court has also been supported by similar decisions of other judges.

During the 1960s, conservation groups added more lawyers to their staffs. In 1967 the Environmental Defense Fund was founded. Its goal was to win legal decisions that would "establish a citizen's right to a clean environment." By the early 1970s a new specialty in law had appeared. Several new journals were devoted to environmental law. In 1971 the *Environmental Law Reporter* devoted thirty-three pages to a summary of federal environmental law. In 1989 the same journal published more than eight hundred pages on the subject.

## THE FIRST EARTH DAY

Despite promising steps and some successes in environmental conflicts, the late 1960s brought plenty of worrisome news to the public. There were reports that fish and other life in Lake Erie were dying from an overdose of nutrients that led to a depletion of oxygen in the water. In addition, one of its tributaries, the Cuyahoga River in Cleveland, was so polluted with industrial chemicals that it caught fire. Oil spills, fish kills, eroded hills—the media reported more disturbing news each week. With each report the general public felt more strongly that the environment was a mess and something had to be done about it. As Denis Hayes, one of the organizers of the first Earth Day, said, "There was this broad, sort of all-encompassing sense that things were falling apart."

Another event, in 1968, also influenced public opinion. The first photographs from a spacecraft were sent back to its home planet. The earth, being covered mostly with water, looked like a blue dot in the black vastness of space. For many viewers this was a powerful image. Astronomer Carl Sagan said, "This blue dot speaks of fragility and vulnerability. It eloquently cries out to us to care for it and cherish it—the only home we've ever known."

At the time only a few politicians in the U.S. government were deeply concerned about the environment. One was Gaylord Nelson, Democratic senator from Wisconsin. He had read *A Sand County Almanac, Silent Spring,* and other books that called for a new relationship between humans and nature. On an airplane in September 1969 he read an article about gatherings called teach-ins, during which people learned about and protested the war in Vietnam. He thought, Why not a national teach-in on the environment?

Using his own funds, Senator Nelson hired a staff to begin organizing the first Earth Day. April 22, 1970, was chosen as the date because most colleges would be in session then; students would not be on vacation or taking exams, and students were a key part of the activities. On that first Earth Day more than ten thousand schools and two thousand colleges and universities held special classes on environmental issues. There were nature walks, litter cleanups, and teach-ins on pollution. In cities there were huge rallies and street

fairs. People of all ages joined in, producing a tidal wave of public concern about the environment.

One person who worked on this national event, Doug Scott, said, "Those of us who organized Earth Day 1970 had no notion of the scale of the event that actually occurred. There was a small crew in Washington that . . . put out a few newsletters and talked to people on the telephone, but it was a very modest effort. What happened on April 22, 1970, was largely spontaneous, and that had an enormous political and social impact, because it said that something just welled up from the people."

The first Earth Day (along with others since) was seen as an opportunity by industries to advertise their good deeds and intentions about the environment. However, such older conservation groups as the Sierra Club and National Audubon Society played a minor role. They were wary of this national outburst of anger and energy about pollution and threats to human health. For their part, some of the new young leaders of environmental groups thought that the conservation organizations—"the birds and squirrels people"—were irrelevant.

Before long, however, the gap between groups that had different agendas narrowed. As Philip Shabecoff wrote in his 1993 history of the environmental movement, *A Fierce Green Fire,* "The cause of reducing pollution and protecting public health was clearly inseparable from the cause of saving the land and preserving nature. The principles of ecology, both scientific and moral, welded the old and the new environmentalism into a movement of fiercely competing but relatively unified national organizations."

IMAGES OF THE EARTH FROM SPACE WERE POWERFUL REMINDERS THAT HUMAN SURVIVAL DEPENDS ON THIS PLANET'S ATMOSPHERE AND NATURAL RESOURCES.

# 4

# From Snail Darters to the Whole World

## (1970–1980)

## THE GOVERNMENT TAKES ACTION

According to Senator Gaylord Nelson, "Earth Day—as was intended—demonstrated to the Washington Establishment and the public that there *was* an environmental movement. The principal and lasting effect was to make environmental concerns a permanent part of the political dialogue in this country."

Even though Richard Nixon, president in 1970, was far from a strong environmental advocate, a torrent of environmental legislation was passed and signed into law during his administration. One was the 1970 National Environmental Policy Act (NEPA). It required that environmental impact studies be made for all federal government projects. The 1970 Clean Air Act and the 1972 Clean Water Act, with goals and regulations for reducing pollution, also became law. The Environmental Protection Agency (EPA) was created in late 1970. This federal agency was a watchdog that oversaw regulation of all sorts of pollution.

Other laws were passed in the early 1970s—the Federal Environmental Pesticide Control Act of 1972, the Noise Control Act of 1972, the Toxic Substances Control Act of 1976, the Resource Conservation and Recovery Act of 1976. Congress also passed laws aimed at giving greater protection to wildlife and wild habitats: The National Parks and Recreation Act of 1978 nearly tripled the amount of land set aside as wilderness in national parks; the Coastal Zone Management Act of 1972 and the Marine Protection, Research, and Sanctuaries Act of 1973 helped protect saltwater life along the coasts and in the oceans; and the Marine Mammal Protection Act of 1972 gave some protection to whales, seals, dolphins, and manatees.

Several other laws dealt with energy issues. The use of energy often yields pollution (including air pollutants and nuclear wastes). So does the production of fuels for energy (which can involve mining wastes and oil spills). Energy is clearly a major environmental issue.

In 1970, at the beginning of the flood of environmental legislation, one vote by Congress was notable because it said no to a proposal. France was building a supersonic aircraft, or SST. The aircraft industry and its allies in

THE CLEAN WATER ACT WAS EFFECTIVE IN REDUCING POLLUTION FROM CERTAIN SOURCES, SUCH AS FACTORY OUTLET PIPES.

Congress urged that the United States build its own SST, with taxpayers absorbing most of the cost. This was exactly the kind of project that Congress usually endorsed. It was new technology, building it would create jobs, and passengers would save travel time. But environmentalists and others raised questions about the effects of waste SST gases on the upper atmosphere; about the harm caused by sonic booms as the aircraft broke the sound barrier; about the wisdom of building something just because it could be done.

In the January 1970 issue of the *Bulletin of the Atomic Scientists,* biologist Garrett Hardin reported that a typical SST flight across North America would save its 240 passengers about two hours of time. A typical flight would also produce a traveling cone-shaped sonic boom that could disturb twenty million people. Was this just the price of progress? Hardin and other environmentalists were asking people to rethink the meaning of the word *progress.*

Later that year approval of a U.S.-built SST was narrowly defeated in Congress. Today the French SST, the Concorde, makes transatlantic flights to airports near the eastern coast of the United States, but flies at subsonic speeds over the U.S. mainland.

Altogether, in the twenty years between 1970 and 1990, the U.S. Congress passed or amended more than fifty environmental laws. Every state also toughened its antipollution laws. Most of these laws, federal and state, were enacted between 1970 and 1980. This span of ten years is sometimes called the Green Decade or the Environmental Era.

## BIG BUSINESS VS. ENVIRONMENTALISTS

The 1970s were the first of three eras, stages, or waves of the environmental movement in the twentieth century. It was a boom time for many environmental groups. Membership doubled or tripled in such organizations as the

Sierra Club and National Audubon Society. New groups formed. The names of some reflected a new global perspective, or homage to the idea of earth as home, earth as mother. Friends of the Earth began in 1970, the Worldwatch Institute in 1974, Earth First! in 1980, Earth Island Institute in 1982.

One of the most significant new environmental groups formed in 1970 with one lawyer and a secretary in a one-room office. Named the Natural Resources Defense Council, it has grown to be a highly effective group that brings legal action on environmental issues. During the 1970s, other environmental groups also added lawyers to their staffs. The Sierra Club established a separate public interest organization, the Sierra Club Legal Defense Fund, "to bring lawsuits on behalf of environmental and citizens' organizations to protect the environment." (This group is now called the Earth Justice Legal Defense Fund.)

The need for increased legal action was great. Even though the general public hoped that all the new antipollution laws were going to erase their worries about the environment, scientists, lawyers, and others in the environmental field saw plenty of trouble ahead. Industries looked for and began to take advantage of loopholes in the new laws. They set to work in state capitals and in Congress, influencing lawmakers to amend laws so as to weaken them. Other tactics were used to discourage the vigorous enforcement of regulations. For example, politicians could boast of voting to give an agency the power to regulate pollutants but fail to increase the agency's budget along with its new responsibilities. Without enough staff the agency couldn't do its job.

At times prodevelopment interests succeeded in making environmentalists look silly in the public eye. For example, in 1977 a controversy arose over building a dam on the Little Tennessee River. The Tennessee Valley Authority (TVA) had begun to build the $136 million Tellico Dam. However, the dam threatened a population of fish, called snail darters, that were known to exist in one small area of the Little Tennessee. The darters had been discovered in 1973, the same year that the Endangered Species Act became law. This act forbids use of any federal funds to harm an endangered species or its habitat.

Citing the act, environmentalists were able to halt the dam for a while, although the loss of a unique species of fish was only one reason to oppose the Tellico Dam. Other objections included the fact that there were several economic alternatives available for the generation of power. Residents of the river valley opposed the dam because they would have to relocate. Cherokee Indians were also against the construction because some of their ancestral homelands would be buried beneath the lake. Moreover, the TVA had already dammed many of the rivers in a seven-state region, so there was plenty of lake fishing and other lake recreation. As a free-flowing river the Little Tennessee offered different kinds of recreation that were becoming scarce in the region.

The TVA searched in vain for other populations of the three-inch-long snail darters. Meanwhile, this agency and other advocates of dam building portrayed the controversy as a simple choice between a beneficial dam and lake and a little fish. Many people believed the choice was that simple.

In 1978 the U.S. Supreme Court upheld the Endangered Species Act and blocked the dam. However, Congress passed legislation that permitted the Tellico Dam to be built. With regret President Jimmy Carter signed this exemption, and the dam was completed in 1979. Soon after, in 1980 and following years, some other populations of snail darters were discovered in Tennessee. Eventually the status of the species was changed from "endangered" to "threatened."

Industries that feared being hampered by the Endangered Species Act exploited the simplistic picture of dam vs. snail darter. The American Mining

THE OPPORTUNITY TO CANOE ON A FREE-FLOWING RIVER WAS ONE OF SEVERAL REASONS ENVIRONMENTALISTS OPPOSED CONSTRUCTION OF THE TELLICO DAM ON THE LITTLE TENNESSEE RIVER.

Congress and the National Forest Products Association, as well as electric utilities, convinced many members of Congress to weaken the law in 1978. Each time the Endangered Species Act is up for renewal, many of the same political forces try to weaken it further.

# THE ACID RAIN CONTROVERSY

In the late 1970s another environmental problem began to draw national—and international—attention. Like most such issues, it pitted industries against environmentalists. It also pitted different regions of North America against one another. The issue was acid rain.

Beginning in the 1950s, scientists had noticed that industrial pollutants in the air eroded the surfaces of buildings and statues and caused fish and other aquatic life to die. In parts of Europe, Canada, and the United States, the rainfall had become more acidic. At a 1972 United Nations Conference on the Human Environment, scientists reported that about three-quarters of the acid precipitation falling on Sweden came from other countries. This was called "a form of unpremeditated chemical warfare."

Research in North America showed that acidic compounds were falling most heavily in New England, northern New York, parts of eastern Canada, and states containing the Appalachian Mountains. The acids fell in all sorts of weather, wet or dry, and sometimes traveled many hundreds of miles before coming into contact with trees, soils, or waters.

Acid rain is a result of burning fuels. While it can come from automobile exhausts and steel mills, the single greatest source is coal-fired power plants. In the 1970s many electric utilities in the United States responded to the Clean Air Act by building very tall smokestacks that dispersed waste gases and particles high in the air. This enabled utilities to reduce local air pollution. In 1973 one coal-burning utility boasted of its tall smokestacks in advertisements. "Waste gases," the utility claimed, "are dissipated high in the atmosphere, dispersed over a wide area and come down finally in harmless traces."

In reality, the "wide area" was narrowed down considerably by the prevailing winds that blow west to east. Research narrowed it further. Eventually scientists were sometimes able to trace a particular fall of acid rain back to its source. For instance, highly acidic rain that fell in central Massachusetts was traced to coal-burning power plants in the Ohio Valley.

The "harmless traces" mentioned in the advertisements seemed to be making lakes lifeless and killing trees. As northern lakes and ponds turned more acidic, most insect life and frogs perished and the abundance and diversity of water life, including plants, declined. This harmed the breeding success of ducks and loons. In the Adirondack Mountains of New York more than half of all high-elevation lakes had abnormally high acidity. No fish survived in most of these lakes. They were still beautiful to look at, but as one person observed, the beauty was all surface, "like cosmetics on a corpse." In Canada the province of Ontario reported 220 lakes that were too acidic to support much life. In the mid-1980s more than 4,000 other Ontario lakes were becoming more acidified.

Spruces, firs, and other coniferous trees that grow at high elevations were also dying or failing to reproduce. In both Europe and North America the most heavily damaged forests grew on high slopes facing prevailing winds. They were most exposed to acid rain and other airborne pollutants.

In the 1980s many environmental groups as well as the Canadian government and the governments of several states called for action to reduce acid rain. The trouble was, acid rain was seen as a regional issue, not a national problem. States that were the sources of most long-range pollutants claimed that tougher air pollution laws would cause huge increases in electricity bills and massive losses of coal miners' jobs. Powerful industries, including coal mining, utilities, and automakers, opposed acid rain reduction. In 1986 these forces led all other lobbying efforts in the amount spent to influence Congress. They exaggerated the amount of money it would cost them to reduce air pollution and argued that acid rain was too poorly understood for any action to be taken.

But as ecologist Gene Likens, one of America's most respected acid rain researchers, said in 1986, "Unanswered scientific questions represent, at most, 20 percent of the obstacle to action on acid rain control. Economic and political factors have always been the main stumbling block."

About that time Likens met with executives of a coal company, to work out differences of opinion. One executive warned him that they had hired a "whole roomful of Ph.D. scientists" to "obfuscate, confuse, and delay the acid rain issue at every opportunity."

Likens was shocked. "Don't you guys care about the human condition?" he asked.

"Of course, but we've got to sell coal" was the reply.

All too often politicians use an alleged lack of information as an excuse of inaction. On the issue of acid rain this was the choice of President Jimmy Carter. Overall he had a good record on environmental issues. (In 1978 he used the Antiquities Act, as Theodore Roosevelt had long ago, to save millions of acres of wildlands, this time in Alaska.) However, in 1979, after calling acid rain a serious environmental threat of global proportions, he announced a ten-year research program. This suited the next president, Ronald Reagan, whose administration (1981–1989) had one of the poorest environmental records of the century.

The acid rain study, called the National Acid Precipitation Assessment Program, cost $600 million and involved two thousand scientists. Partway through the study, in 1987, a progress report was issued. It was sharply criticized by many scientists. The report's conclusions seemed to be tailored to match the goal of the Reagan administration—to do nothing about acid rain. The Canadian government called the report "voodoo science." Actually most of the science was solid but was misrepresented by the report's conclusions, written by the research program's manager, Lawrence Kulp. He soon resigned.

The final report, issued in 1990, was less biased but still lacked important information, especially about the long-term effects of acid rain on soils and forests. Overall there was plenty of evidence, as there had been ten years earlier,

RECENT RESEARCH ON ACID RAIN SHOWS THAT POLLUTION MUST BE REDUCED EVEN FURTHER IF LAKES IN PARTS OF THE EASTERN UNITED STATES AND CANADA ARE TO SUPPORT LIFE AGAIN.

that something needed to be done about acid rain. Pressure from environmental groups and from the general public finally led to some action during the administration of President George Bush. The Clean Air Act was revised, with new regulations aimed at reducing emissions of sulfur dioxide, the main cause of acid rain. In 1991 the United States and Canada also agreed to fight acid rain and other pollutants on both sides of the border.

A key part of the revised Clean Air Act allowed power plant owners to choose among several ways to reduce pollution. They were not required to install costly devices called scrubbers that remove most sulfur from the waste gases of coal-burning plants. They could burn cleaner fuels or promote the efficient use of electric power so less would be needed. They were given incentives for exceeding their targets for reducing pollution. The Environmental Defense Fund (EDF) was mainly responsible for these novel ways of helping utilities reduce pollution without huge expense. (In its lobbying against acid rain controls, the electric utility industry claimed the annual cost would exceed $11 billion. The actual cost in the late 1990s was about $1 billion a year.) When President Bush signed the law, he commended EDF and other environmental groups "for bringing creativity to the table to end what could have been a hopeless stalemate."

By the mid-1990s there was evidence that the most common pollutant (sulfates) in acid rain was decreasing. However, another pollutant (nitrates) had not lessened. Moreover, a long-term study of a New Hampshire forest revealed that acid rain had apparently changed soil chemistry enough to cause trees to stop growing. In 1998 Gene Likens said, "We still have a major problem with acid rain. That is scientific fact." The Clean Air Act called for cutting pollution further after the year 2000. Yet, with stronger evidence of harm caused by acid rain, environmental groups urged that utility smokestack emissions be cut even more.

# CONTINUING CONCERNS

The acid rain issue illustrates some of the challenges faced by the United States and other nations. The flurry of new laws during the Green Decade of 1970–1980 tackled many visible threats to human health. Usually the remedy was to make the offending industry install pollution controls. Some laws contained more than five hundred pages of very specific details. The goal was to ensure compliance, to leave no loopholes. However, these rigid command and control laws, as they were called, discouraged creative ways of solving problems. Sometimes it seemed that large sums of money would have to be spent to achieve a very small reduction in pollution. This fueled the resistance of businesses and of some politicians who wanted to dismantle many environmental regulations.

By 1980 the great optimism of Earth Day 1970 and the early 1970s had been replaced by the reality that environmental problems were far from being solved. In fact, the very agencies that had been established to reduce pollution and improve the overall environment sometimes had to be sued in order to force them to take action. Furthermore, a new generation of problems was emerging. Some threatened the well-being of all life on earth.

# 5
# New Challenges
## (1980s)

The greatest single achievement of this most scientifically productive of centuries is the discovery that we are profoundly ignorant: we know very little about nature and we understand even less.

—Lewis Thomas, *Amicus Journal*
(Summer 1981)

## STALEMATES AND SETBACKS

The early years of the Reagan administration were like a slap in the face of the environmental movement. Ronald Reagan believed that he had a mandate to get government "off the backs of the people." This meant easing or ending antipollution rules and giving private industries easy access to the resources on public lands. In his book *A Fierce Green Fire,* environmental journalist Philip Shabecoff wrote: "In some ways, the Reagan administration appeared to seek a return to the robber baron, survival-of-the-fittest capitalism of the nineteenth century."

The budget of the Environmental Protection Agency was slashed. By 1985 it was about that of a decade earlier (with inflation increases accounted for). Government grants for research on energy conservation and solar energy were ended. The Forest Service and other agencies that administer public lands were given new chiefs who favored increased logging, mining, and grazing.

As secretary of the interior James Watt carried out the policies of President Ronald Reagan. This made him a favorite target of editorial cartoonists.

Reagan appointed James Watt head of the Department of the Interior. Watt was a lawyer and former lobbyist for the U.S. Chamber of Commerce. He had headed the Mountain States Legal Foundation, a group that fought to gain access to the resources of public lands. Watt saw no point in saving resources for future generations. According to his religious beliefs, the Second Coming of Christ would occur soon, and with Judgment Day almost here, he thought it was pointless to conserve resources. He advocated oil drilling off the California coast and encouraged westerners to exploit the resources of public lands, including wilderness areas.

Anne Gorsuch Burford was appointed head of the Environmental Protection Agency. At the EPA she refused to meet with environmental leaders; her key advisers came from chemical, automobile, and petroleum companies, the very industries whose pollution the EPA was supposed to regulate. One of her early goals was to weaken the agency's law enforcement division.

Ronald Reagan believed that environmentalists were a fringe group. In reality the President was on the fringe. He and his allies in the business world were out of touch with the feelings of U.S. citizens about the environment. Millions of people signed petitions or called for the removal of Watt and Burford. (Both resigned in 1983.) The antienvironmental actions of the Reagan administration inspired many to become more involved in environmental issues. Thanks to Watt, Burford, and Reagan, membership in national environmental groups rose dramatically, from about four million in 1981 to seven million in 1988.

In Reagan industry leaders thought they had found the leader of an antienvironmental counterrevolution. Instead they discovered that Congress was strong enough to resist most attempts to weaken laws and actually voted to strengthen some, including the Clean Water Act. Moreover, state governments strengthened their environmental efforts to make up for the lack of federal leadership and action.

Still, environmentalists look back on the Reagan administration as eight lost years. The United States had been a global leader on environmental issues. In the 1980s its government became an obstacle to progress. Nor did the situation improve much after 1988, when Reagan's former vice president, George Bush, was elected president.

## GLOBAL CHALLENGES

The 1980s were a decade of stalemate. At times this second stage of the environmental movement was just a holding action, as environmentalists, and the American public, tried to hang on to earlier gains. The 1990s brought a new era. Environmental leaders recognized that some antipollution laws had been poorly planned and were both difficult and costly to carry out. They saw a need for more flexible ways of solving environmental problems. (The plan for reducing acid rain was an example of this kind of solution.)

Environmentalists also saw that cooperation among nations would be needed to solve some problems. Tropical forests were being destroyed at the rate of six acres a minute. With them whole habitats containing species of animals and plants unknown to humans were being destroyed. The stocks of edible fish in the oceans were being rapidly depleted. Furthermore, people, with their own fast-growing numbers and their new technology, were changing the vast ocean of air, the earth's atmosphere, in ways that could cause great harm to life on earth. None of these problems could be solved by the United States or any nation acting alone.

The problems were challenging enough, but environmentalists also faced increased resistance from industries and their political allies. This was shown in the conflict over taking action to prevent global warming and to stop the thinning of the earth's ozone shield.

## THE OZONE HOLE DEBATE

A layer of ozone in the stratosphere blocks most dangerous ultraviolet light from reaching the earth's surface. Without this ozone all life on land would perish. Loss of some of the ozone would allow more ultraviolet light to pass through, causing skin cancer, cataracts, damage to human immune systems, and harm to many other forms of life.

In 1970 a Dutch chemist, Paul Crutzen, working in Germany, found that certain chemicals might harm the ozone layer. In 1974 two U.S. chemists, Sherwood Rowland and Mario Molina, discovered that chlorine from compounds called Chlorofluorocarbons (CFCs) could destroy ozone. A single chlorine atom could destroy a hundred thousand ozone atoms.

CFCs had been considered harmless. They were widely used, particularly as coolants in refrigerators and air conditioners. They were also used as propellants in spray cans and as cleaning solvents of electronic circuit boards. CFCs were the basis of an $8 billion industry.

Scientists around the world reported evidence that supported the Rowland and Molina ozone depletion theory. (In science a theory is not a mere idea or hypothesis. For an idea to be called a theory it must be supported by evidence.) The use of CFCs in spray cans was stopped. Scientists and environmentalists began to call for a ban on all CFCs. They were called doomsayers and un-American by the threatened industries and by others opposed to government regulation. These forces went to extraordinary lengths to attack the scientific evidence supporting the ozone depletion theory, including hiring scientists to defend CFCs.

Atmospheric scientists and chemists continued to find evidence that supported the theory. In 1985 a thinning of the ozone shield over Antarctica was reported. This ozone hole, as it was called, was later confirmed to be evidence that chlorine from CFCs was eroding the earth's ozone shield. Nevertheless, opponents of regulation continued to challenge the evidence. Some claimed, incorrectly, that gases from a volcano caused the Antarctic ozone hole.

In addition to attacking scientific evidence, defenders of CFCs claimed that there were no good substitutes and painted a grim picture of the economic blow that would result if they were banned. However, CFC manufacturers were quietly developing substitutes. When a series of international agreements led to a phasing out of CFC use, the manufacturers of these chemicals were actually able to cut production earlier than required. As for the huge cost of substitutes, consider the case of Texas Instruments. In 1989 the cost of materials, including CFCs, for a single cleaning process of circuit boards was more than $350,000. In 1995, when a process without CFCs was used, the cost was just $14,000.

---

PEOPLE ONCE THOUGHT THAT THERE WAS A LIMITLESS SUPPLY OF FISH IN THE SEA. NOW WE KNOW THIS IS NOT SO.

In the 1990s the amount of harmful ultraviolet rays reaching the earth increased, especially in southern Chile and Argentina. The ozone hole over Antarctica grew larger, and reached record size—nearly three times the area of Europe—in 1998. However, it was expected to shrink gradually and return to normal by about 2050 because fewer and fewer CFCs were entering the atmosphere. In 1995 Paul Crutzen, Sherwood Rowland, and Mario Molina won the Nobel Prize in chemistry for discovering the chemical threat to the ozone layer. Later that year the United States and Europe stopped making CFCs.

By 1998, 150 countries had signed the Montreal Protocol—the agreement to phase out the use of CFCs—and also had agreed to phase out the use of some other chemicals that are ozone depleters. This was unprecedented global cooperation on an environmental problem. The remaining challenge was for wealthy nations to help developing nations pay some of the costs of changing processes that still used CFCs.

Remarkably, despite all this progress, in the late 1990s there were still members of Congress proposing laws that would force the United States to resume making and using CFCs. Some media talk show hosts also refused to accept the fact that CFCs caused any problem. They said that the science behind the ozone depletion theory was "debatable." In a sense that is true. Everything in science is debatable. That is a basic strength of science; ideas can be challenged and even changed when convincing evidence is found or developed. On the matter of vanishing ozone, however, no such evidence was offered.

HIGH ABOVE THESE ICE CAVES ON ROSS ISLAND, ANTARCTICA, ARTIFICIALLY MADE CHEMICALS HAVE CREATED A VAST THINNING OF THE PROTECTIVE OZONE LAYER OF THE STRATOSPHERE.

# THE THREAT OF GLOBAL WARMING

In addition to trying to prove that CFCs were not responsible for the thinning of the ozone layer, foes of regulation attacked the scientific basis for concern about global warming. The oil, coal, auto, and utility industries in particular opposed any change. They funded scientists and others who challenged the evidence that human activities were causing the entire atmosphere to warm. As is often the case, most of the scientists who criticized the evidence were not experts on the workings of the earth's atmosphere. With a few exceptions, the world's atmospheric scientists agreed that global warming was real.

The earth's climate has warmed, and cooled, many times before. Just eighteen thousand years ago glaciers up to two miles high covered most of North America and northern Europe. The earth has warmed considerably since then. The giant glaciers melted, and sea levels rose.

For nearly all of those eighteen thousand years since the last glaciers, and for many years before that, the atmosphere had a fairly steady amount of carbon dioxide, about 275 parts per million. Carbon dioxide is given off by living things as a waste gas. It also enters the atmosphere when trees, animals, and other organic things decay or burn. Carbon dioxide plays an important role in making the earth a livable planet. It and other gases such as methane and water vapor absorb heat from the sun. They're called greenhouse gases.

The amount of carbon dioxide in the atmosphere began to rise in the late 1700s, at the beginning of the Industrial Revolution. Since then, as more and more coal, oil, natural gas, and wood have been burned, carbon dioxide levels have risen. Today manufacturing, the use of automobiles, the clearing of

RISING TEMPERATURES HAVE CAUSED GLACIERS AND PERMAFROST TO MELT IN THE ARCTIC. FURTHER WARMING MAY THREATEN THE SURVIVAL OF POLAR BEARS AND OTHER WILDLIFE LIVING THERE.

forests, and other human activities add several billion tons of carbon dioxide to the atmosphere each year. Carbon dioxide levels have reached 360 parts per million, higher than at any time in human history. In the twentieth century the earth's temperature increased about one degree Fahrenheit.

A single degree of temperature rise may seem insignificant. However, those giant glaciers of eighteen thousand years ago were brought about by temperatures just nine degrees colder than today's. A change of a few degrees can have dramatic effects. For example, rising temperatures cause water to expand.

BURNING OF FOSSIL FUELS ADDS BILLIONS OF TONS OF CARBON DIOXIDE TO THE EARTH'S ATMOSPHERE EACH YEAR.

In the past few decades the global sea level has risen several inches, enough to cause increased damage during coastal storms. On land there are other signs of a warming earth. The Arctic is growing steadily warmer. Spring comes earlier, and the southernmost permafrost is beginning to melt. Glaciers all over the world are retreating. On some mountains trees near the timberline that normally have stunted growth because of cold are growing tall and fast.

Humans may cause the earth's temperature to rise several degrees in the twenty-first century. If this happens, rising sea levels will inundate coastal regions, large parts of Florida, and some low-lying islands. Global warming will also change weather patterns in ways that are still not well understood. Agriculture will be affected. Some countries may benefit, with an improved climate for crops. Others may suffer from crop-killing droughts. Another likely effect of global warming will be an increase in the severity and frequency of storms, including hurricanes.

Our understanding of the earth's atmosphere has grown quickly, but scientists admit there is still much to learn. Nevertheless, about global warming, "There is no debate among statured scientists of what is happening. The only debate is the rate at which it's happening," said James McCarthy, an atmospheric scientist at Harvard. The important question, according to McCarthy, is not if the earth is warming; it is. The most important unknown is how sensitive the climate is to disturbances and how its growing instability is likely to disrupt our planet and our lives.

With the exception of a few scientists who receive research grants and other funding from the oil and coal industries, atmospheric scientists worldwide agree that steps should be taken to reduce the amount of carbon dioxide and other greenhouse gases entering the atmosphere. They were not encouraged much by the results of the 1997 Kyoto Protocol, in which thirty-eight industrialized nations agreed to cut their emissions by about 5 percent by the year 2012. For the United States the goal was a 7 percent reduction. (The United States leads the world in greenhouse gas emissions, with 25 percent of the total.) Even if these goals are achieved, the gains will probably be wiped out by rising emissions of greenhouse gases from such developing nations as China and India.

Atmospheric scientists and environmental groups saw the Kyoto Protocol as a small first step. However, some of the general public probably wondered why any action was needed. Many people believed there was serious debate among scientists about the reality of global warming. Television news reports helped create this notion. To give an appearance of balanced reporting, two scientists might be quoted, one a spokesman for industry, the other an atmospheric scientist. This "balance" is misleading.

According to Ross Gelbspan, author of *The Heat Is On,* "The reason most Americans don't know what is happening to the climate is that the oil and coal industries have spent millions of dollars to persuade them that global warming isn't happening." The American Petroleum Institute spends nearly as much for public relations as the entire budget of the top five U.S. environmental groups.

Industries continue to spend heavily to impede international negotiations like those at Kyoto and to try to discredit the scientific evidence on global warming. However, beginning in the 1990s, one industry began to heed the evidence and the warnings of scientists. It was the insurance industry, which suffered from an increase in the frequency and severity of storms.

During the entire decade of the 1980s insurers paid $17 billion for weather-caused losses worldwide. Then, in just five years—1990–1995—it paid $57 billion for such losses. Many insurance companies became convinced that global warming played a role in the increase of floods, hurricanes, and other weather disasters. They concluded that the threat of global warming is real. At a 1996 international conference on global change, sixty insurance companies signed a statement urging the world's nations to reduce greenhouse gases.

Some environmentalists saw some hope in this wake-up call for the general public. The insurance industry, which relies on the best evidence available to set the rates and terms of its policies, had begun to worry publicly about the catastrophic losses that global warming might bring.

While powerful industry groups continued to claim that steps toward reducing greenhouse gases were unneeded and would be a huge expense, experts

MANY INSURANCE COMPANIES HAVE CALLED FOR ACTION TO HALT GLOBAL WARMING. THEIR RESEARCHERS BELIEVE THAT IT IS ALREADY CAUSING AN INCREASE IN TORNADOES AND OTHER WEATHER DISASTERS.

in the energy field pointed out that great reductions in these gases could come cheaply from using more energy-efficient machines and processes. According to energy expert Amory Lovins of the Rocky Mountain Institute, some companies were not waiting for government action. In 1999 he wrote: "They're becoming very clever in finding new ways to turn climate protection into profits, and are committed to doing it vigorously. . . . U.S. leadership on climate protection has quietly passed from the public to the private sector."

Nevertheless, U.S. leadership was needed to achieve global cooperation in bringing a halt to the warming of the atmosphere: a situation that begged for action, not delay.

## CONSERVATIVES AND CONSERVATION

On the issue of global warming and other environmental problems, attacks on the credibility of scientists and scientific evidence comes from politicians, columnists, talk show hosts, and others who call themselves conservatives. This has led to questions about the true meaning of that term. The words *conservative* and *conservation* have the same root. *To conserve* means "to keep from being damaged, lost, or wasted." To be conservative is to be prudent and cautious. Today people who call themselves political conservatives do tend to resist change, but does this make them true conservatives?

Conservative people think long range. They do not spend their life savings on impulsive luxury vacations. Conservative people invest for the future, for themselves and their children and grandchildren. Conservative people are careful to maintain equipment and other belongings, whether they are their own cars and homes or a company's machinery. These same values were applied to the use of resources by President Theodore Roosevelt, a Republican *and* a conservationist.

These values are exactly the opposite of those held by some who call themselves conservative today. When natural resources are at stake, these "conservatives" think short term. Exploit the resources now; worry about any consequences later. If these "conservatives" had enough political power, manufacturers would be free of bothersome regulations, and the air and waters would be a dumping ground for wastes.

Today's "conservatives" also support corporate welfare, which rewards certain businesses with tax breaks and cheap access to public resources. For example, ranchers pay far below fair market value for grazing rights on western public lands. Timber companies also receive corporate welfare when public funds are used by the U.S. Forest Service to build and maintain logging roads. On private lands logging companies have to bear the cost of the roads they need.

In 1993 environmental journalist Philip Shabecoff wrote that the Reagan administration's so-called conservative philosophy was actually "an odd amalgam of libertarianism and corporate socialism." In 1996 biologist and author Dr. Edward O. Wilson of Harvard University spoke about these so-called conservatives: "They're not conservatives at all. They're radical libertarians. . . . That strain of thinking is not conservatism in the traditional sense. . . . At its core, conservatism is the preservation and wise use of our resources and tradition."

Who are the real conservatives? Those who oppose environmental safeguards and conservation of resources or environmentalists who strive to conserve the natural world for generations to come?

# 6

# Many Shades of Green

## (1990s)

Despite its potential, environmentalism has yet to exercise its power decisively. Possibly it may never do so. The forces that oppose it—a minority, to be sure, but one that possesses enormous wealth with which it can exercise control over the nation's political and economic affairs—have given ample evidence that they will not lightly surrender their power.

—Philip Shabecoff, *A Fierce Green Fire* (1993)

## ENVIRONMENTAL GROUPS, BIG AND SMALL

In the United States opinion polls show that more than eight out of every ten people say they are environmentalists or support environmental goals. This means that environmentalists come from a broad range of society. They come from different ages, races, religions, occupations, and political parties.

They are not, as some critics claim, elitists, wealthy people who want to preserve their way of life and block further progress for others. Actually the label of "elitist" more readily fits opponents of environmentalism. The core of anti-environmentalism is made up mostly of top business leaders, almost all of them wealthy white males.

On the signs in the image:
"150 decibels of noise is enough to drive a man insane. Midtown New York is 77 and rising."
"April 22 is Earth Day. The beginning of the end of poll..."

"It's a good thing we don't have to drink the Hudson River."
"...th Day. The beginning of the end of pollution."

ENVIRONMENTALISTS COME FROM A BROAD RANGE OF THE POPULATION. MANY ARE MEM-
BERS OF LOCAL GRASSROOTS ORGANIZATIONS.

Although it is true that the leaders of national environmental groups are mostly well-educated white males who earn upper-middle-class incomes, the top-level staffs of these groups include many women. Also, in the 1990s these national groups increased their efforts to recruit members of minorities for their staffs. Furthermore, the total membership of these groups represents only about a third of the environmental movement. An estimated twenty-five million people belong to one or more environmental groups. Most are members of local grassroots organizations, and in these, women and minorities are better represented than in the large national groups.

Grassroots groups exist in cities, towns, and counties all across the United States and Canada. Usually these organizations have no ties to big national groups. Like the Scenic Hudson Preservation Conference (see page 51), local groups form to deal with local problems or issues. It may be to save a marsh or other valuable wildlife habitat from development. It may be to fight to reduce pollution or remove a toxic dump. It may be to try to keep some facility—a landfill, an incinerator, a shopping mall—from being built. The ultimate issue may be health and safety, or it may be the overall quality of life where people live and work. American history shows that great changes do not usually begin with political leaders; they usually begin in the streets and local communities.

Many of these local efforts came to be labeled "NIMBY," meaning "not in my backyard." Although this attitude can reflect selfish, narrow-minded opposition to any nearby change, often it reflects ordinary people fighting for a better environment. It challenges the old notion that any project that creates jobs and yields tax revenues should be built. In every community this notion is often supported by some business groups and construction unions, so NIMBY activists face opposition. However, NIMBY efforts often bring most of a community together in a common cause.

The membership of both local environmental groups and well-known national organizations has ups and downs. Beginning in 1992, membership in some national groups declined after the election of Bill Clinton as president, partly because the new vice president, Al Gore, had a strong environmental record as a senator. The people whom President Clinton chose to head the EPA, the Department of the Interior, and other key agencies also marked a sharp, positive change from the Reagan-Bush administrations. When people have reason to hope for action from the federal government, their contributions to national environmental groups usually drop.

Support for environmental groups rose again in 1995, when the 104th U.S. Congress took office. This was because the 1994 elections put several antienvironmentalists into positions of power. Encouraged by Speaker of the House Newt Gingrich, a far-ranging attack on environmental laws began. Committees started rewriting, and weakening, environmental laws, sometimes with direct help from industry lawyers and lobbyists. One Republican senator introduced a bill that would have wrecked the Endangered Species Act. Word soon leaked out that the bill had been written by lawyers for the timber industry and other businesses that would gain by reduced protection of public lands. This news helped prevent passage of the legislation.

Attempts were made to weaken many other laws that regulated water pollution, forest management, grazing, and pesticides. However, the industries and their political allies soon learned that the American people weren't interested in dismantling laws protecting the environment. They had mistaken complacency for indifference. A million people signed a petition for an "Environmental Bill of Rights" that was presented to Congress on Earth Day 1995. Environmental groups, both national and grassroots, worked together as never before. They also formed coalitions with other groups. For example, environmental groups joined with health and labor organizations to defeat a proposed law that would have weakened efforts to enforce environmental, consumer protection, and job health and safety laws.

A key step in the overall environmental effort was to draw the attention of the news media to this sneak attack on environmental laws. Major newspapers belatedly began to report that industry lawyers were helping rewrite laws that the general public did not want changed. Members of Congress began to hear from voters back home. In 1995 almost all the antienvironmental legislation was defeated. Once again the people of the United States showed that one of their core values is concern about the environment.

Nevertheless, some Republicans came to another conclusion: that they had failed to explain their antienvironmental efforts well enough. So "explaining" environmental issues to the general public has come to be seen as an important goal of those who seek to weaken environmental laws or block new ones.

## "Green" Education

One sector of the population getting increased attention from industry groups is young people. The reason for this is obvious. Many schools have ecology or conservation clubs. Usually these groups do not just study issues; they take political action—in their schools, communities, or states. Most of their actions are not controversial—planting trees, caring for a local patch of wildlife habitat, promoting recycling, cleaning up beach litter.

However, sometimes actions like these can have political impact. For instance, in 1989, a California high school student named Allen Graves was among several young people receiving an award at the White House in Washington, D.C. Graves was being honored because of his efforts to get recycling started in his school and community. He asked President George Bush, "Does your office recycle?"

SOMETIMES THE CONCERNS OF CHILDREN LEAD THEIR PARENTS TO BECOME ACTIVE IN ENVI-
RONMENTAL ISSUES.

The president replied, "I don't know."

Graves said, "It should," and eight months later the White House began to recycle paper and cans.

Some student actions, like boycotting products and writing accusatory letters to politicians, may stir controversy—and opposition. In the mid-1990s there was a backlash against environmental education in schools. Thirty-one states require some environmental education; some also require special environmental training of teachers. Unlike many other subjects, learning about the environment tends to encourage people to change their behavior and that of their culture. This upset some conservative groups and businesses. They claimed that textbooks and other environmental materials for children were biased, erroneous, and incomplete. They charged that children were being indoctrinated with dangerous environmental myths.

Critics of "Green" education cited examples of factual errors and misleading statements in textbooks. Even the most ardent supporters of environmental education agreed that there were flaws in some textbooks. However, Karen Schmidt, a staff reporter of *Science* magazine, wrote: "Environmental educators say the charges are overblown: Although critics will always be able to dredge up anecdotes that highlight questionable teaching practices, they say, most schoolchildren are being taught sound lessons on how nature works and how human activities affect the planet."

A forest economics expert examined many school materials on forestry issues and came to a surprising conclusion: A booklet published by the Sierra Club was more scientifically accurate than many textbooks. This was true in general: Information provided by such environmental groups as the Sierra Club and National Audubon Society was more balanced than that contained in textbooks. Nevertheless, the goal of some conservative critics of environmental education is to tip the balance in favor of the industry view, saying, for example, that global warming is "just a theory."

In 1997 Carl Pope, executive director of the Sierra Club, wrote: "It is ironic that the same conservative movement that laments the erosion of traditional values in American education should object to environmental education programs that teach thrift (turn out the lights), personal responsibility (recycle your trash), and civics (write your congressman). These values are all just fine, it seems, unless they are tied to real-world problems like global warming."

## How Big Business Influences Students

In addition to attacking "Green" education, industry groups have stepped up their efforts to get materials presenting their viewpoint into schools. Dan Barry, the director of the Clearinghouse on Environmental Advocacy and Research, said, "We consider this the cultural war of the environmental movement. Corporations understand that many Americans have learned their environmental awareness from their children, so now they want to insert their logic into the schools and at home."

Businesses, including electric utilities, have for decades had educational programs aimed at schoolchildren. The sponsoring organizations and businesses include the oil companies Exxon and Mobil, the American Coal Foundation, Dow Chemical, International Paper and other timber companies, and the American Nuclear Society.

The booklets, videos, posters, and coloring books supplied by businesses can be useful in teaching, but all favor their corporate sponsors when it comes to environmental issues. In doing so, they are often inaccurate and misleading. The companies and groups call their free materials educational; others call them propaganda. More than a hundred samples of "sponsored educational materials" were analyzed by Consumers Union, publishers of *Consumer Reports.* The study found that about 80 percent contained blatant bias, commercial pitches, inaccuracies, or often all three.

Many students need a teacher's help to spot the hidden messages in these materials. To be fair, they also may need help in spotting inaccuracies and oversimplification of environmental issues in their textbooks. Unfortunately many teachers are either too busy or lacking in knowledge about environmental issues to be of much help. Some naively accept the messages in corporate-sponsored materials as truthful and use them in their classrooms.

## GREENSCAMMING AND ASTROTURF GROUPS

Business groups and others opposed to environmental regulations use various tactics to confuse the general public. A favorite ploy is to create an antienvironmental organization but to give it a name that leads people to believe it is an environmental group. This is called greenscamming. In the 1990s dozens of groups across the nation had environment-friendly names that masked antienvironment agendas. One of the first, founded in 1953, was Keep America Beautiful, Inc., "dedicated to litter prevention and improved waste handling practices." This group has vigorously opposed mandatory recycling laws and some effective ways of reducing litter, for example, laws that require a deposit on beverage containers so people are encouraged to return them for recycling. Keep America Beautiful, Inc., supports any litter prevention effort that does no economic harm to its main sponsors: can and bottle manufacturers, brewers, and soft-drink bottlers.

If an antienvironmental group presents itself as a local grassroots effort, it is called an AstroTurf organization, after the artificial grass. Examples of AstroTurf organizations in California include Friends of Eagle Mountain. This group was created on behalf of a mining company that wanted to use an abandoned mine pit as a landfill. Another, the Alliance for Environment and Resources, supported the goals of the timber industry. Also in the West, the goal of Northwesterners for More Fish was to limit federal efforts to protect endangered fish species in the Columbia and other northwestern rivers if the efforts might interfere with businesses that use the river. These included electric utilities, aluminum companies, and the timber industry. Oil, mining, and chemical companies were also involved in this group, which had no workable plan for actually helping fish populations.

Many of the state and regional antienvironmental groups are part of a loose confederation called the wise use movement. (In the 1980s a similar coalition was called the sagebrush rebellion.) According to Ron Arnold, director of the Center for the Defense of Free Enterprise, the goal of the wise use movement is simple: "to destroy, to eradicate the environmental movement." In 1992 the newsletter of one wise use group, People for the West!, accused environmentalists of having "a plan to list more and more plants and animals as endangered, add more wilderness, and pass federal laws that make it impossible to mine, harvest, graze livestock, and even recreate on public lands. It's a scheme to remove people from public lands in America!"

Although People for the West! calls itself a grassroots organization, in 1992 twelve of its thirteen directors were mining industry executives.

National antienvironmental organizations include Citizens for the Environment. Despite its name, this group has no ordinary citizens as members; it is an industry group that has fought passage of air pollution laws. The National Wilderness Institute was formed to weaken laws protecting endangered species. The National Wetlands Coalition favors the draining, filling, and development of marshes and other wetlands.

## MISLEADING ADVERTISEMENTS

About the time of the first Earth Day in 1970, businesses discovered the value of advertisements and public relations efforts that boasted of their environmental good deeds. Major public relations companies created new departments to help their corporate clients present themselves to the public in the best "Green" light. However, the truth behind the advertisements is quite different. Almost without exception, the "earth-friendly" action an oil company or other industry boasts about is required by law—perhaps to reduce pollution or to protect the habitat of an endangered species. The company probably fought to prevent the law from being enacted, and, chances are, its lobbyists are still at work trying to influence legislators to weaken the law's regulations. In the meantime the company, still obliged to comply with the regulations, advertises its good environmental deeds.

One example is the advertisements that appeared in the mid-1980s from Chevron, an oil and gasoline company, that boasted of efforts made to protect an endangered species of kit fox. The actions were the kind any industry has to agree to before being permitted to operate in the habitat of an endangered species. At the same time, Chevron was a member of the American Petroleum Institute, a lobbying group fighting environmental regulations. In 1996 Herb Gunther, president of a public relations firm that works for public interest groups, said, "The ads celebrate something their lawyers fight tooth and nail to prevent. . . . Those ads are a vile form of propaganda."

Big business is not the only one that slants information in order to influence people. Environmentalists also sometimes select, exaggerate, or omit information in advertisements and public statements in order to make a convincing case. Some environmental groups have more credibility than others. The most respected and influential groups have well-trained, respected scientists on their

INDUSTRIES SOMETIMES BOAST ABOUT GOOD DEEDS THEY ARE ACTUALLY REQUIRED TO DO—BY LAWS THEY TRIED TO DEFEAT.

staffs because they realize that an understanding of ecology and other sciences is the basis for wise environmental policies, and that in environmental conflicts, scientific expertise is a source of power.

In 1995 the National Audubon Society announced that it was "recommitting" itself to science as a foundation for its work. It hired a new director of science "to build a culture of science" in the organization. The leadership of this national group understood that accuracy was crucial in all of its work. Basing its policies on accurate information would bring greater credibility and respect.

## RADICAL ENVIRONMENTALISTS:
## HELP OR HINDRANCE?

There is a variety of major national environmental organizations in the United States. Some are more radical in their attitudes and actions than others. Different groups sometimes join forces to fight for a common goal, but usually each one focuses on different environmental problems. For example, one of the

A WORKER FOR THE NATURE CONSERVANCY STUDIES SATELLITE PHOTOS IN ORDER TO HELP ESTABLISH PARK BOUNDARIES IN GUATEMALA. THIS ENVIRONMENTAL ORGANIZATION HELPS MANY NATIONS PROTECT RAIN FORESTS AND OTHER VALUABLE WILD HABITATS.

most respected environmental groups is the Nature Conservancy. Its primary goal is to save biodiversity (the rich variety of living things) by protecting habitat. With nearly twelve hundred employees and thousands of volunteers, it manages a nationwide system of more than sixteen hundred nature preserves that total more than 7.5 million acres. It also has a strong international program that helps other nations protect wild places.

Besides buying some sites directly, the Nature Conservancy cooperates with state governments. Sometimes it is able to buy a special habitat, saving it from development in the nick of time because a state government cannot act quickly enough. Later the state buys the land from the conservancy and protects it as a park.

The single largest environmental group, with more than four million members, is the National Wildlife Federation. Like most major groups, it includes on its staff experts in biology, toxic substances, forestry, fisheries, and other natural resources. Once a coalition of sportsmen's clubs, the federation eventually opened its membership to any person, and ordinary concerned citizen members came to outnumber outdoorsmen. The National Wildlife Federation is far from a radical organization, but its large membership makes it an effective force in politics. When it took the unusual step of calling for the resignation of James Watt in 1981, his days in Washington were numbered.

There are radical environmentalists and groups that look with disdain at the big national organizations. They feel as David Foreman, a founder of Earth First!, did when he once said, "Too many environmentalists have grown to resemble bureaucrats—pale from too much indoor light; weak from sitting too long behind desks; co-opted by too many politicians."

Greenpeace, the Sea Shepherd Conservation Society, Earth First!, and other grassroots radical groups sometimes commit illegal acts in the name of

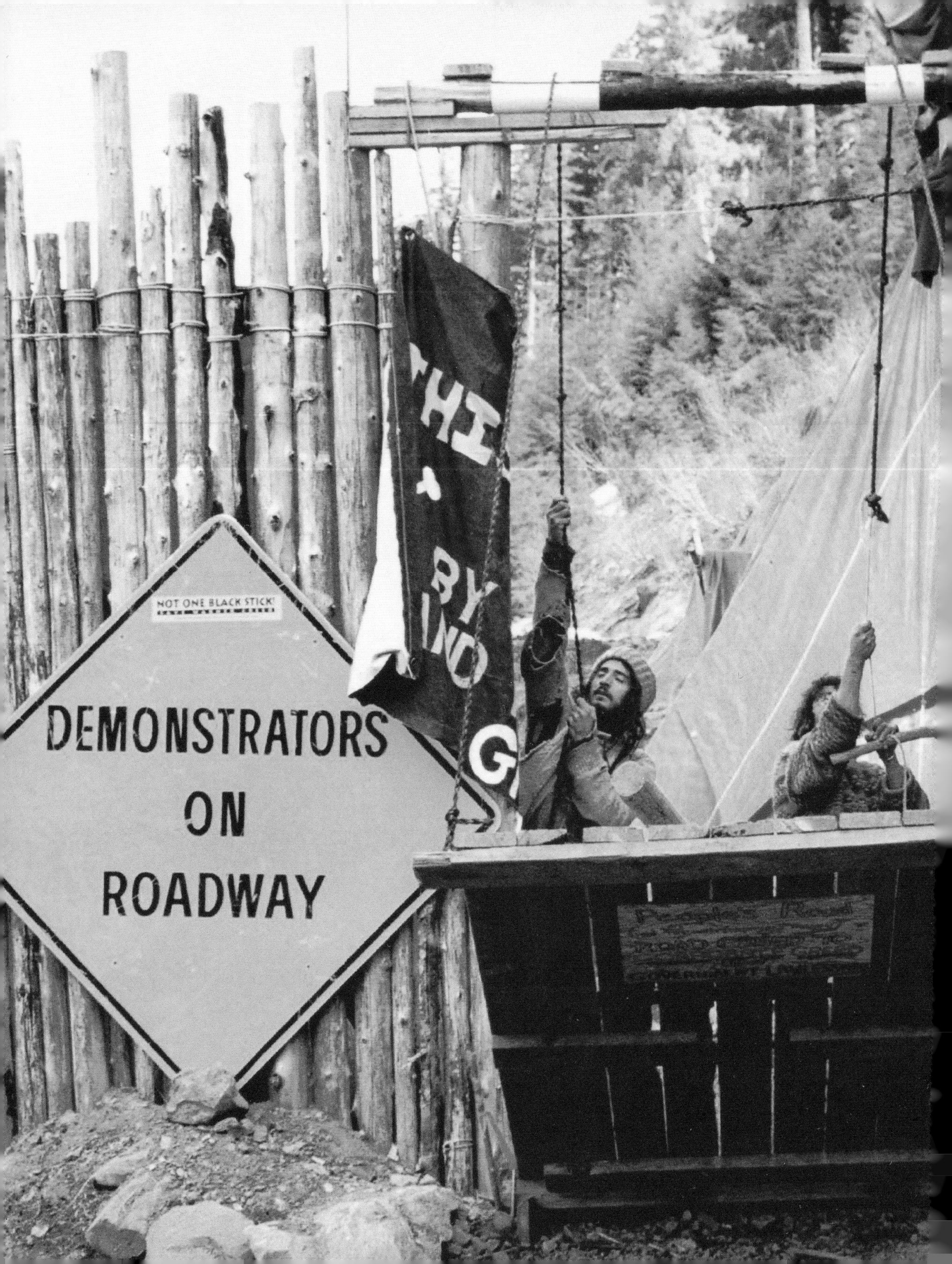
NOT ONE BLACK STICK
DEMONSTRATORS
ON
ROADWAY

environmentalism. These have included interfering in whaling, timber cutting, and nuclear testing. They do these things because they think that direct action is sometimes the only way to make the public aware of the issues involved. In 1995 a Greenpeace spokesman said, "Confrontation is critical to get coverage in the press or to reach the public some other way."

On the other hand, the companies that are the targets say that radical environmentalists try to arouse emotions with misinformation and scare tactics instead of using facts and the law to make a case. Some environmentalists agree. A spokesperson for the Wilderness Society pointed out that Greenpeace tended to look for ways to publicize problems instead of ways to solve them.

RATHER THAN WORK THROUGH THE COURTS OR CONGRESS, RADICAL ENVIRONMENTALISTS SOMETIMES USE EXTREME METHODS. (HERE THEY ARE BLOCKING ROADS TO HALT LOGGING IN OREGON'S WILLAMETTE NATIONAL FOREST.)

In 1998 and 1999 an underground group called Earth Liberation Front (ELF) claimed responsibility for several acts of ecoterrorism. It burned several buildings of a Colorado ski resort and a forestry industry office in Oregon. Some of ELF's statements suggested it was more of a radical animal rights group than an environmental organization. The Sierra Club and other environmental groups condemned ELF's actions.

Significantly, David Foreman, a founder of Earth First!, is no longer connected with that group. While he continues to believe radical organizations do some good, he thinks they are not really effective at achieving environmental goals. In 1998 he said, "I've never changed my goal as a conservationist—and that's to protect as much wilderness and as many intact ecosystems and native species as possible. And as times change, as a person changes, you seek new ways of doing that." Since 1991 Foreman has led the Wildlands Project. It aims to establish buffer zones around parks and refuges and wild corridors between preserves in order to help the survival of wildlife, particularly large species. This involves working cooperatively with landowners, both private and public—a far cry from the sometimes illegal actions of Earth First!

Considering the many shades of Green—the variety of environmental groups—some disagreements are inevitable. Sometimes the leadership and membership of a group are divided. That occurred within the Sierra Club in 1998. This organization is unusual in that its members vote by mail to elect its board of directors and to approve club policies. In 1998 there was a proposal on the ballot that the club work toward achieving a stable U.S. population, partly by restricting immigration. A supporter of this proposal warned that unless U.S. population growth was slowed, "many laudable environmental initiatives will amount to little more than mopping the floor while leaving the spigot on."

The club's board of directors put a counterproposal on the ballot. It reaffirmed the group's position of urging an end to world population growth but took no position on U.S. immigration policies. Carl Pope, the club's executive director, said of the anti-immigration idea, "It is offensive to people of color, even those who think we should limit immigration. The Sierra Club cannot protect our environment by building a wall around our borders." This view was supported in the election; the anti-immigration proposal was defeated.

## THE GAIA HYPOTHESIS

Among the more radical-thinking environmentalists are people who advocate the Gaia hypothesis: that the earth is a living organism. (Gaia is the name of the Greek goddess of the earth.) First proposed in 1972, this hypothesis states that the outer shell of the earth—its crustal rocks, lands, oceans, and atmosphere— and the life on it are part of a single ecosystem. The conditions on the earth's surface—especially the composition of the air and the temperature of the planet's surface—are regulated by the activities of all living things. Of these living things, such organisms as bacteria and algae, not large animals, are most vital because they play crucial roles in the recycling of earth's elements and in maintaining the earth's oxygen supply.

Although evidence has been found to support the Gaia hypothesis, it is not widely accepted by scientists. There are many uncertainties. This provides opportunity for people to misinterpret it and try to use it to advance their own causes. Some antienvironmentalists have used it to argue that the earth can adjust to all sorts of pollution and disruption by humans. Some environmentalists have used it in the opposite way to argue that the earth is fragile.

Scientists who support the Gaia hypothesis say that, yes, the earth can adjust to huge disruptions and atmospheric changes. Several times in its history it has done so after asteroids have hit the planet and caused widespread extinction. But while the earth can adjust, the adjustment may well be disastrous for humans. "The idea that we are wrecking the earth is wrong; but wrecking ourselves is another story," said microbiologist Lynn Margulis, the leading proponent of the Gaia hypothesis in the United States.

## THE ANIMAL RIGHTS MOVEMENT

Among those who call themselves environmentalists are some who believe in deep ecology, a philosophy in which humans are seen as no more important than trees, birds, or other living things. This is similar to the philosophy of the animal rights movement. Of course there is diversity in that movement as well, but the most radical believers oppose all use of nonhuman animals and consider the welfare of a deer, rabbit, or goose nearly as important as that of a person.

This view is not shared by most people in the United States and Canada. Because of this, some animal rights and animal welfare groups claim to be conservation or environmental groups in order to broaden their appeal. Sometimes they join forces with mostly environmental groups to further a common cause. In 1998, for example, the Humane Society of the United States (usually considered an animal welfare or animal rights group) joined the Sierra Club, the Center for Marine Conservation, and several other environmental groups in a campaign to urge greater protection of sea turtles.

Conservative politicians and others who seek to discredit environmentalists try to lump together the environmental and animal rights movements. Environmental groups fight this because there are fundamental differences between the two movements. Animal rights advocates are usually concerned about the well-being of every individual animal, as if it were a pet or a child. For the most part their arguments are emotional, and their statements are often not supported by scientific evidence.

In contrast, environmentalism is rooted in ecology and other sciences. There are, of course, emotions involved too, but environmental positions are usually well supported by scientific evidence. Ecologists are most concerned about the well-being of species and populations, not individual animals. In nature it is normal for many individual animals to die while the overall population thrives. This is why such respected environmental groups as the National Audubon Society and Defenders of Wildlife do not oppose hunting. In fact, people who hunt and fish were the foundation of the conservation movement, and today they are the natural allies of environmentalists on most issues.

Asked whether environmentalists should embrace the animal rights movement, two Sierra Club members responded in the July–August 1994 issue of *Sierra.* One said: "The animal rights movement's view of nature too often seems based on Bambi cartoons—all emotion and simplification." The other warned that an alliance with the animal rights movement—"hysterical, fuzzy-thinking, and irrational—would bring discredit to environmentalism, which has been unfairly characterized as having the same flaws."

In the eyes of the public, in state capitals, and in Congress, the environmental movement has earned respect and credibility by usually backing its claims and policies with solid information. Whatever it may accomplish in the future will depend on its having both passion *and* credibility.

# 7

# Toward the Future

## (INTO A NEW CENTURY)

The crisis is not long-term but here and now; it is upon us. Like it or not, we are entering the century of the environment, when science and politics (governments and other institutions) will give the highest priority to settling humanity down before we wreck the planet.

—Edward O. Wilson, *Science* (March 27, 1998)

## FAR-REACHING EFFECTS

The environmental movement, born in the United States, has influenced people all over the world, although China and other developing nations are just beginning to confront the harm that pollution does to the health of their citizens. In Western Europe environmental activists not only work from outside government, as in the United States, but have also formed Green parties and been elected to seats in parliaments.

In the United States concern about the environment has had many effects. Some are now taken for granted by nearly everyone. Others might still be considered radical. Consider, for instance, a housing project completed in Cambridge, Massachusetts, in 1998. There are forty-one apartments, but the residents cook meals, dine, and do laundry in one communal building. There is also a community garden. A heat pump provides heating and cooling.

Because of energy-efficient windows and other choices of building materials and design, the homes use 60 percent less energy than conventional construction. Many parts of the buildings, including glass tiles in the bathrooms, are constructed of recycled materials. The insulation is made from recycled newspapers.

As one resident said, recalling a nearby neighborhood where she had lived, "There's such a duplication of resources. I used to think about it as I walked my kids around the neighborhood. Why were there twenty snowblowers and twenty washing machines between us?"

While most people in the United States and Canada are probably not ready to join such a community, even the private houses they dream of having are not the energy hogs they once were. Community building codes do not allow it. In design, materials, plumbing, and appliances, newly constructed houses have become less wasteful of energy and water. This is just one way in which the environmental movement has changed everyday life in the United States and other industrialized nations.

Another change brought about by the environmental movement is the mandatory recycling laws many cities and towns have passed. Huge volumes of newsprint, magazines, glass, metal cans, and many kinds of plastic are collected for reuse in new products. Moreover, the market for recycled materials has grown, sometimes with help from the government. Early in his administration President Bill Clinton ordered all federal agencies to buy paper containing a significant percentage of recycled paper. This was a big boost for the recycled paper market.

Concern about the environment has also affected the content, engineering, packaging, and even shape of some products. For example, the streamlined shapes of automobiles reduce friction with the air and improve gasoline

mileage, thereby reducing air pollution.

Another change, now taken for granted, is revealed in the newsletters and other inserts that accompany bills from utilities. Before the 1970s electric and gas utilities urged consumers to use as much energy as possible. Now they give tips on using less and on buying energy-saving appliances. They may even give rebates or other incentives to encourage people and companies to conserve energy. Between 1977 and 1997 these efforts cut peak electricity demand by more than twenty-one thousand megawatts nationwide. That's the output of forty-two new power plants—expensive projects that utilities did not have to build. In addition, by burning less coal and natural gas to produce electricity, utilities reduce the amount of carbon dioxide and other greenhouse gases going into the atmosphere.

Environmental concerns also affect the decisions of all sorts of governments, from the smallest community all the way to Washington, D.C. There is no doubt that the laws and regulations have had positive effects. In every state there are examples: a toxic waste site cleaned up, factories emitting less pollution, reduced pollution in rivers and lakes. There are many success stories.

## Too Bright an Outlook?

A controversial book published in 1995 celebrated the achievements brought about by environmentalists. Titled *A Moment on the Earth: The Coming Age of Environmental Optimism,* it was written by magazine reporter Gregg Easterbrook. More than seven hundred pages long, this book described significant progress in the quality of the environment and chided environmentalists for being negative. They are "doomsayers" that "pine for bad news" when in truth, according to Easterbrook, the major environmental battles have been won.

The book was praised by reviewers in some magazines and newspapers, and its message delighted the forces in and out of Congress that were trying to weaken environmental laws. It also pleased industries that had the same goal. An advertisement of the Mobil Corporation, for example, raved about the book. It was headlined THE SKY IS *NOT* FALLING.

However, reviewers in scientific journals and environmental magazines had other views. For one thing, the book contained scores of factual errors. To judge by the weight of evidence from wildlife biologists, climatologists, and other scientists from around the world, Easterbrook's optimism was based on wishful thinking, not facts. "The major problem is that these happy ruminations, soothing as they may be, simply do not accord with the facts," wrote Peter Raven, director of the Missouri Botanical Garden and an expert on biodiversity.

David Orr, chairman of the environmental studies program at Oberlin College, cited another flaw. Writing in *Natural History,* he said that the author's optimism "rests on a foundation of political naivete. . . . *A Moment on the Earth* has virtually nothing to say about human arrogance, greed, stupidity, and evil— all of those things that keep people and whole societies from doing what they can do and what they ought to do."

Environmental leaders acknowledged that progress had been made and should be hailed and celebrated. Some types of air and water pollution had been sharply reduced. Industries in the United States had greatly cut their releases of toxic chemicals. However, in the late 1990s, 40 percent of the nation's rivers and lakes were not fit for drinking, fishing, or swimming. The air quality in many cities was still not healthy—not for the general public and especially not for people with asthma and other breathing difficulties.

Carol Browner, head of the EPA in the Clinton administration, said, "While we've done a lot, the challenges of tomorrow are going to be far more complicated." Water pollution is an example. Great effort was needed to reduce wastes coming from such large sites as factories and wastewater treatment plants. That was largely accomplished. Now it is a much greater challenge to reduce the runoff of fertilizers, silt, and pesticides from countless scattered farm fields and housing developments.

In 1998 environmental groups began to sue state and federal agencies to meet that challenge. Citing a dormant provision of the Clean Water Act, the environmentalists used the law to open a new front in the struggle to reduce water pollution. Of course the regulatory agencies could have acted at any time, but they had to be pushed into action. Oliver Houck, director of Tulane

University's environmental law program, said, "Nothing works in environmental law unless citizen pressure forces the regulators to move on the regulated entities. It is like a fish nipping at a fish nipping at a fish."

Decades of work by environmentalist also resulted in altered U.S. Forest Service policy. Many Forest Service employees had petitioned for change. Timber has always been sold cheaply to the logging industry while waterways and wildlife habitat are given inadequate protection. Michael Dombeck, chief of the Forest Service in the second term of President Clinton, suspended the construction of logging roads on thirty-three million acres of land. Dombeck pointed out that the agency had a road maintenance backlog of $8.5 billion and a budget for that purpose of less than $600 million a year. He also banned mining on two national forests located along the wildlife-rich Rocky Mountain Front.

## THE LOSS OF BIODIVERSITY

Another challenge—and perhaps one of the greatest—that all humanity faced at the dawn of the new century was loss of wild habitats and their biodiversity. In the United States one of the first triumphs of conservationists was the protection of such wild places as national parks and national wildlife refuges. People thought that the wildlands and waters, and all the life in these habitats, were saved. Eventually it became clear that lines on a map don't always protect a preserve. The survival of the unique ecosystem within the borders of Everglades National Park, for example, continues to be threatened by human mismanagement of the flow of water into the park.

Ecologists have learned that saving parks, even large ones, is not enough to protect wildlife and plants from extinction. Such large mammals as elk, bison, and wolves do not stay within park limits and may run into trouble outside the park. Even smaller species gradually die out within parks that are like islands in a sea of development. In Oregon the river otter, ermine, mink, and spotted skunk died out in Crater Lake National Park. In Utah the red fox, spotted skunk, and white-tailed jackrabbit disappeared from Bryce Canyon National Park. At least eleven native mammal species no longer live in Washington's Mount Rainier National Park.

The greatest losses were in the smallest parks. This means that parks should be bigger and, even more important, have surrounding buffer zones in which some kinds of development are barred. Bruce Babbitt, secretary of the interior in the Clinton administration, said, "We cannot protect the splendor and biological diversity of the natural world by simply fencing off a few protected areas within an overall landscape of exploitation."

In the 1990s many people learned that conservation laws in the United States and Canada were not enough to protect migratory songbirds. In Central and South America the usual wintering habitats of some kinds of warblers, thrushes, and other species were fast disappearing. In addition, some species were vulnerable to widespread use of biocides, including those banned from use in the United States. Grassland birds, including meadowlarks and bobolinks, were especially hard hit.

Some of the blame for the decline of songbird numbers was aimed at coffee growers. Traditionally, coffee bushes had been grown in the shade of other trees. These forests were vital habitat for orioles, warblers, and hummingbirds, as well as many insects, lizards, and other wildlife. But in response to a growing market for coffee, farmers in Latin America had been switching to high-yield plants that grow in full sun.

In 1997 the National Audubon Society and the Smithsonian Migratory Bird Center began promoting a brand of coffee, Cafe Audubon, that was certified as being grown in traditional shade plantations. This was the reverse of a

CHANGES IN THE WAYS COFFEE BEANS ARE GROWN CAN HAVE AN IMPACT ON MIGRATORY BIRDS AND OTHER LIFE. THIS IS JUST ONE EXAMPLE OF HOW THE GLOBAL ECONOMY CAN AFFECT THE ENVIRONMENT.

boycott, in which consumers are urged to shun a product. "By selecting Cafe Audubon," the publicity read, "you link yourself with farmers who are practicing good land stewardship and protecting birds." By creating a market for shade-grown coffee, environmentalists sought to influence coffee growers to reverse the trend toward full-sun coffee farms.

About the same time, environmental groups began working with candy companies that were concerned about world supplies of the cacao bean from which chocolate is made. To satisfy the world's great hunger for chocolate, growers had been carving large plantations out of rain forests. Despite the use of pesticides and fertilizers, many plantations failed. Plantation cacao trees seem more vulnerable to diseases and pests than trees that grow naturally under taller trees.

Researchers and chocolate makers began to understand that the future of cocoa lies with small farmers using more shaded, forested sites. The goal, they agreed, was sustainable farming—that is, taking good care of one site instead of abandoning it and using much less fertilizer and pesticide. This pleased environmentalists because research has shown that small, naturally shaded cocoa farms are like shade-grown coffee farms—havens of biodiversity, including migratory songbirds.

Although there are still plenty of local and national environmental issues in the United States, there are growing numbers like the coffee and chocolate examples. It is sobering to recognize that choices made in a supermarket can have a large environmental impact thousands of miles away. It is disturbing for people to realize that their consumption of coffee or chocolate could help determine whether they will hear the flutelike song of a wood thrush next spring.

As worrisome as global warming was, the ongoing and accelerating loss of biodiversity was seen by most biologists as the greatest environmental problem of the twenty-first century. Humans were causing the fastest mass extinction of living things in the 4.5 billion-year history of the planet. In 1996 Edward O. Wilson said, "All of the other problems, like overheating the globe for a period, vicious little wars, nuclear terrorism—these may be forgotten in the centuries ahead, but not the depletion of biodiversity. That's the one irreversible thing."

Wilson added, "My gut feeling is optimistic. . . . We're moving toward an era of environmental awareness that could be widespread and intense enough to make a difference."

## STRIP-MINING THE OCEANS

At the dawn of the new century it became clearer and clearer that humans were affecting the earth's resources in unprecedented ways. Consider ocean fish, a crucial source of food for the earth's growing population. Improved ships, equipment, and ways of locating fish had made it possible for the overall catch of seafood to grow. In the views of some economists, this was proof that environmentalists were too negative.

However, looking at a year's total catch can give a false picture of the condition of the world's fisheries. A comprehensive study of global fish catches from 1950 to 1994 was published in 1998. It showed a gradual shift from long-lived predatory fish (at or near the top of food chains) to short-lived fish that fed on plankton (at or near the bottom of food chains). While this shift increased the total catch, it threatened the survival of many species of edible fish. The study found that 60 percent of the world's most commercially valuable species were overfished or fished to the limit. One result: Fish like herring that had once been considered a bait or trash species had begun to show up on restaurant menus and in seafood shops.

One researcher, Daniel Pauly of the University of British Columbia, said, "Present fishing policy is unsustainable. The food-web structure is changing. . . . If things go unchecked, we might end up with a marine junkyard dominated by plankton." To avoid widespread fisheries collapse, scientists urged that large "no-take" marine protected areas be established. This would require extraordinary cooperation on the part of the nations with fishing fleets.

The remarkable thing about this crisis in the world's fish stocks is that nations probably *would* cooperate, and fish populations would have a chance to recover. This would not have happened a few decades ago. Now, however, people realize that humanity does have the power to wreck the ocean's fisheries. They realize that the warnings of scientists and environmentalists are not "fear-mongering" but are based on trustworthy information.

## UNDOING THE DAMAGE

Research by ecologists and other scientists has given us a better understanding of the workings of nature. Near the turn of the new century government agencies began to put some of this wisdom to work, often to undo the damage caused by earlier government projects. In May 1996, for example, the U.S. Bureau of Reclamation released 117 billion gallons of water from Lake Powell, allowing it to roar down the Grand Canyon. This was the kind of flood that used to scour the valley of the Colorado River before Lake Powell formed behind the Glen Canyon Dam. The flood had positive effects on the river valley habitat and probably on populations of native fish that suffer from the lack of natural floods. The long-term effects of this human-made flood were being studied, partly to determine how often to release such an extraordinary flow of water.

Some environmentalists advocate getting rid of the dam and Lake Powell entirely, to restore the natural flow of water through the Grand Canyon. This seems unlikely to happen, but in 1997 a dam in Maine was ordered demolished by the Federal Energy Regulatory Commission. The Edwards Dam on the Kennebec River generated hydroelectric power but produced just one-tenth of 1 percent of Maine's electricity. Meanwhile it blocked salmon, sturgeon, and other fish from reaching spawning grounds. A broad coalition of environmen-

IN 1996 BILLIONS OF GALLONS OF WATER WERE ALLOWED TO SURGE DOWN THE COLORADO RIVER IN AN ATTEMPT TO BRING ABOUT THE GOOD EFFECTS OF THE RIVER'S FORMER ANNUAL FLOODS.

tal groups as well as state and federal wildlife agencies had gathered evidence and argued to have the natural flow of the Kennebec River restored. In the twenty-first century, hundreds of other dams will be judged by whether they do more harm than good, with some being torn down.

Several other states also took steps to restore natural river flows. In the 1950s the Army Corps of Engineers had changed 103 miles of Florida's meandering Kissimmee River into 56 miles of straight canal. The goal was to reduce floods and drain wetlands for farming. The result was a disaster for fish, birds, and other wildlife and no end to floods. In 1992, prodded by the Sierra Club, other environmental groups, and the state of Florida, the Corps of Engineers began to undo its costly work—for an estimated $370 million—filling in much of the canal with dirt and reopening some of the river's twisty course.

In California too efforts were made to get rid of dams and levees and to let rivers run as free as possible. In 1998 voters in the Napa Valley, California, approved a plan to rip out flood control structures and halt costly and ineffective dredging on the Napa River. Low-lying areas that were part of the river's normal floodplain were to be abandoned and become marshes and other valuable wildlife habitat.

The most ambitious and costly water project by far was an attempt to undo the damage done to the Florida Everglades ecosystem. It would take fifteen to twenty years and cost at least $8 billion. The Everglades region, including Everglades National Park, was dying after decades of drainage, altered water flow, and pollution. Populations of egrets and other wading birds were down 90 percent. The numbers of deer, turtles, and many other animals had dropped at least 75 percent below normal. The water supply of several Florida cities was threatened, as were fish and other marine life in Florida Bay.

One of the first steps toward rescuing the Everglades was taken in 1997,

HUMAN MISMANAGEMENT HAS DISRUPTED THE NATURAL FLOW OF WATER IN THE EVERGLADES REGION, HARMING WILDLIFE POPULATIONS AND WATER SUPPLIES. IT WILL COST AT LEAST $8 BILLION TO UNDO THE DAMAGE.

when the Clinton administration and the state of Florida agreed to buy more than fifty thousand acres of sugarcane fields near the national park. This step was aimed at stopping some of the flow of fertilizers, pesticides, and other pollutants into the park. Another action, begun in 1998, was to buy out fourteen hundred landowners so that normal water flow could be restored to six thousand acres west of Miami. Further steps, still being planned, involve getting rid of many canals and levees in an attempt to restore much of the natural water flow of the Everglades.

Currently the United States is the leader in trying to correct the folly of past river and wetland projects, but similar projects are being studied in other countries as well. In Romania and Ukraine wetlands of the Danube River delta are being restored. Many thousands of acres of drained land are becoming wetlands again in the belief that fish, other wildlife, and natural flood control are more valuable than farmland.

In addition to reclaiming rivers and wetlands, there are scores of projects across North America aimed at restoring habitats, including prairies, forests, and salt marshes. There are also efforts to restore populations of mammals and birds in suitable habitats. Atlantic puffins were lured back to establish a breeding colony on an island off the Maine coast. In California common murres had been wiped out in one area of the central coast by an oil spill. They too were lured back to reoccupy several islands. River otters were released in rivers and streams of western New York after more than a century of absence.

Most dramatic of all, wolves were restored to Yellowstone National Park in 1995 and 1996, when thirty-three Canadian wolves were released there. They have reproduced and are thriving. The wolf was the lone native species that had been killed off in the Yellowstone ecosystem, and ecologists and environmentalists campaigned for many years to bring it back. The environmental group Defenders of Wildlife helped allay some of the concerns of nearby ranchers by offering to pay market value for any livestock wolves might kill. The group made the same offer in 1998, when Mexican gray wolves were released in national forests along the Arizona–New Mexico border.

## COOPERATIVE EFFORTS FOR A COMMON CAUSE

In the twenty-first century there will be increased efforts to return native species to areas where they once lived. There will also be greater cooperation among landowners, environmentalists, and government agencies in trying to solve problems. Late in the twentieth century there were some remarkable agreements on land use issues that could serve as models for the future. One affected the future of biologically rich "sky island" mountains; another involved thousands of square miles in southern California.

The so-called sky islands are forty mountains in northern Mexico, southern Arizona, and southern New Mexico. They and their surrounding landscapes are home for an incredible diversity of life. The area is a mix of public lands and more than thirty privately owned ranches. The ranchers used to distrust environmentalists but joined with them in the common cause of improving the range and preventing it from being divided into house lots. The Malpai Borderlands Group is the name given to this alliance of ranchers, the Forest Service, and the Nature Conservancy. They work together to prevent overgrazing, restore native grasses, and protect endangered species.

On a much larger scale, environmentalists, land developers, and government officials worked in the San Diego area for six years to create a plan for saving native plants and animals, many of which exist only in southern California. The plan called for adding to wild habitats that were already set aside. In exchange for giving up rights to develop large natural areas, developers were freed of any obligation to protect species on other lands. It was a creative way to apply the Endangered Species Act.

Some environmentalists believed that the plan was too generous to developers. Many supported it, however, as well as its extension to all of southern California. This was the United States' most ambitious attempt to reconcile land development and nature preservation. In 1997 Secretary of the Interior Babbitt said, "I consider the plan the latest and best example of a new era in American conservation. Voluntary conservation partnerships on private lands will be as important to America's natural heritage in our children's lifetimes as President Teddy Roosevelt's founding of the National Wildlife Refuge system and establishment of new national parks and national monuments in the early twentieth century was to us."

## NATURE OR JOBS?

For every hopeful sign that environmental goals can be met through cooperation with private developers and businesses, there are other signs of fierce opposition to them. In 1998, for example, plans of oil companies to oppose any action to reduce global warming were revealed. The plans called for spending $5 million to find scientists who would support the industry's position, then to train them in public relations so they could convince journalists, politicians, and the public that nothing should be done about global warming. Whether this effort would succeed is doubtful. Many journalists and ordinary citizens considered such scientists to be about as credible as those who work for tobacco companies and say that the harmfulness of smoking has not been proved.

Despite these plans of the oil industry, there were some hopeful signs as the millennium approached that people put less stock in some simplistic claims of those who oppose environmental regulations. One of the most basic was this simple choice: nature or jobs, or, as John Muir once put it, "beauty or bread." In other words, if environmental regulations were imposed on industry, then productivity, profits, and employment would suffer.

This idea was expressed in a blunt bumper sticker in the Pacific Northwest during the early 1990s: "Save a Logger, Kill an Owl." The owl referred to is the northern spotted owl, a species threatened with extinction and one reason why environmental groups and the U.S. Fish and Wildlife Service opposed the logging of old growth forests. Although there were many reasons to save some of what little was left of this unique ecosystem, the timber industry and most news media left the public with the idea that protection of a few hundred owls was the only issue and that a proposed ban on logging would cause great harm to businesses, workers, and communities. In fact, in the 1992 campaign President George Bush warned that "we'll be up to our neck in owls, and every mill-worker will be out of a job."

However, two years later a *New York Times* article about the results of protecting the forests said that "economic calamity has never looked so good." The economy was thriving, even in the counties that were most dependent on the timber industry. True, timber-related jobs had been lost, but in many cases this was a result of overall trends in the industry toward mechanization and increased export of logs. Industry workers who lost their jobs quickly found other employment in a thriving economy.

Economists have investigated the matter of jobs vs. nature nationally. They found some situations in which specific regulations had short-lived effects on certain industries, communities, and jobs. Overall the pursuit of environmental quality does not hinder economic growth and development, and the question "Nature or jobs?" presents a false choice. In 1994 Mollie Beattie, director of the Fish and Wildlife Service, said, "There's only one conflict, and that's between short-term and long-term thinking. In the long-term, the environment and the economy are the same thing—if it's unenvironmental, it's uneconomic."

## The Green GNP

For many years the practice of traditional economics has upset environmentalists—and conservationists before them. In a landmark essay published in the *Bulletin of the Atomic Scientists* in 1970, biologist Garrett Hardin drew contrasts between two sciences, ecology and economics. He wrote that while researching nature, the ecologist "studies all inputs and outputs, regardless of who pays for them or who benefits from them." Economics, which Hardin called "the handmaiden of business," was different. It did not include all inputs and outputs. Some things were called external costs, or externalities. These were often negative, harmful effects that were borne by nature or by people. Nevertheless, in traditional economics these externalities were ignored. Hardin wrote that "the myth of 'externalities' must be abandoned." He predicted that "ecology will engulf economics. The more inclusive science will encompass the less inclusive."

By 1990 researchers who called themselves ecological economists were challenging traditional economics. They accused economists of mismeasuring development, underestimating the hard-to-measure costs of development, and ignoring the long-term effects of development. In the Netherlands an economist named Roefie Hueting devised a new way for each nation to tally its gross national product (GNP), a measure of the total output of goods and services. His plan, which is sometimes called the Green GNP, accounted for the harm that economic activity does to the environment. It should replace the traditional ways of measuring GNP, he said, and "demonstrate how we are squandering air,

SURVIVAL OF THE NORTHERN SPOTTED OWL WAS JUST ONE OF MANY REASONS ENVIRONMENTAL GROUPS OPPOSED LOGGING OF SOME OLD GROWTH FORESTS IN THE PACIFIC NORTHWEST.

water, ground, spaces, silence, as if they were free goods instead of assets that we are losing."

In traditional economics, a rising GNP is considered a good sign—that a country's economy is improving and its people are better off. Its forests, soils, air

quality, and other natural assets may be deteriorating, but these losses are not subtracted from the GNP. When money is spent to combat pollution and its effects, that money is counted as a plus. Thus the $2 billion spent to clean up the mammoth *Exxon Valdez* oil spill of 1989 created a rise in the GNP of the United States. Similarly, Americans spend $40 billion a year in health care expenses as a result of air pollution. That figure is counted as a plus too. The nation would certainly have been better off without the oil spill or the illnesses caused by pollution, but the traditional way of calculating GNP suggests otherwise.

In the new century some form of Green GNP will probably be adopted because the research of ecological economists has produced further proof that the traditional GNP should be changed.

## NATURE'S GOODS AND SERVICES

Earth's life support system is taken for granted, but the normal functioning of nature provides humans with vital services that are usually unappreciated until they are lost. In 1998 a team of scientists and economists from several nations tried to figure out the value of ecosystem services—goods and services that nature provides to people worldwide (see pages 128–129). They concluded that replacing ecosystem services would cost a mind-boggling amount: $33 trillion a year. That's about double the GNP of all nations on earth.

The researchers said that the exact sum was not important; recognizing the value of ecosystem services was. As economist Lawrence Goulder of Stanford University said, "Having this number calls people's attention to the fact that ecosystem services are absolutely essential to human life, and that there's no price we could pay that would be enough."

People do not usually think of ecosystem services. As Worldwatch researcher Janet Abramovitz observed, "We are like young children who think

that food comes from the refrigerator, and who do not yet understand that what now seems free is not." Many still believe that progress and prosperity are not dependent on nature. In a 1997, speech zoologist Jane Lubchenco, president of the American Association for the Advancement of Science, said, "As humans fill in wetlands, clear-cut forests, degrade coral reefs, drive natural populations and species to extinction, and introduce alien species, we often disrupt the functioning of the systems or lose the ecosystem entirely. When we do, we begin to incur unanticipated and occasionally staggering costs—having now to manufacture, grow, or otherwise provide what we once got for free."

MARSHES, SWAMPS, AND OTHER WETLANDS WERE ONCE CONSIDERED NUISANCE AREAS TO BE DRAINED OR FILLED IN. NOW THEY ARE RECOGNIZED AS VITAL PROVIDERS OF ECOSYSTEM SERVICES.

# ECOSYSTEM SERVICES

*biological control*             predator control of prey species

*climate regulation*             of greenhouse gases in the atmosphere

*cultural values*                aesthetic, artistic, spiritual,
                                 educational, and scientific values

*disturbance regulation*         storm protection, flood control, and
                                 drought recovery

*erosion control and sediment storage*   prevention of soil loss by water
                                         and wind; storage of silt in lakes
                                         and wetlands

*food production*                production of fish, game, crops,
                                 nuts, and fruits by hunting, fishing,
                                 gathering, or subsistence farming

*gas regulation*                 balance of oxygen and carbon
                                 dioxide in the atmosphere; ultraviolet
                                 protection from ozone

*genetic resources*              genetic materials from nature that help
                                 provide new medicines and improved
                                 food plants

| | |
|---|---|
| *nutrient cycling* | provision of nutrients for new life; removal of nitrogen from the air and its conversion to a form that living things need |
| *pollination* | making possible the reproduction of many plants |
| *raw materials* | production of lumber, fuels, and fodder |
| *recreation* | provision of sports fishing, bird watching, tourism, and other forms of outdoor activities |
| *refuges* | provision of nurseries for vulnerable young, habitats for migratory species |
| *soil formation* | weathering of rocks into soil; buildup of dead organic materials |
| *waste treatment* | clearing up of pollution; detoxification of dangerous substances |
| *water regulation* | provision of water for irrigation, mills, and transportation |
| *water supply* | provision of water by watersheds, reservoirs, and aquifers |

An example of the unappreciated value of nature's services comes from the water used in New York City, well known for its purity and good taste. Most of the water comes from reservoirs in the Catskill Mountains, where forested surroundings help filter and purify it—just one of the ecosystem services provided by the forested land. In the early 1990s some development in the area brought agricultural runoff and sewage into the water. New York City had a choice. One solution was to build a water purification plant, at a cost of $6 billion or more, plus annual operating costs of $300 million. The other was to spend about $1 billion to buy more than thirteen thousand acres of land and take other steps to reduce pollution entering the reservoirs. The city government chose the latter, spending much less money to help nature continue to provide its vital services.

Economists debated about how knowledge of ecosystem services could be used in the twenty-first century, but there was growing agreement that steps had to be taken to halt the destruction of nature. Sustainability was the goal: using nature in ways that preserved its ability to provide its vital services far into the future.

## To the Future

In the twentieth century first the conservation movement, then the environmental movement changed and grew tremendously. Early in the century it focused on saving some wild places and wildlife; late in the century it was challenging the economics profession to start keeping accurate accounts of what various human activities and projects *really* cost.

The term *environmentalist* came into use when human health issues and pollution were added to the traditional conservation issues. By the beginning of the new century the list of environmental concerns had broadened further. It included economics, social justice, and national security.

Whether in an industrial or a developing country, poor people and poor communities often bear the main burden of a degraded environment. They get the polluting factory or the toxic dump and are not well prepared to defend themselves in the political system. However, in the 1990s both grassroots and national environmental groups began advocating environmental justice. This will be an increasingly important issue in the twenty-first century.

National security is also an environmental issue. Scarcity of resources, and competition for them, can lead to wars, revolutionary movements, and economic chaos. In a 1997 speech U.S. Secretary of State Madeleine Albright said: "Environmental problems are often at the heart of the political and economic challenges we face around the world. . . . We would not be doing our jobs as peacemakers and as democracy-builders, if we were not also good stewards of the global environment."

In the twenty-first century the environmental movement will grow in worldwide influence. It will confront many issues but none greater than the loss of earth's rich biodiversity and the far-reaching threat of global warming. Solutions to these problems will depend on people switching from oil and coal to alternate energy sources, and to unprecedented cooperation among environmental groups, businesses, and nations.

The concerns of the environmental movement have grown. So has its strength, as it has become more ingrained in the values of people and has gained credibility from the support of scientists worldwide. As one scientist, the world-renowned entomologist Edward O. Wilson, said, "Environmentalists have been looked on as the dreamers of the world, when in fact they are the realists."

The environmental movement will need every bit of its strength and help from every person who calls himself or herself an environmentalist as it faces the challenges of the new century—the century of the environment.

# Environmental Groups and Agencies

Today there are thousands of environmental groups in the United States and Canada alone. Many are small and focus on local or state issues. For example, the Mono Lake Committee works to protect this unusual lake in eastern California. Some with nationwide membership have a narrowly focused goal. The North American Bluebird Society, for instance, aims to increase bluebird populations.

Other environmental organizations are large and work on a national or even an international level, though they may also have local chapters. The major groups publish magazines that are sometimes available in public libraries. For example, *Sierra* is published by the Sierra Club, and *Audubon* by the National Audubon Society. You can learn about their aims and efforts by reading these periodicals.

Listed on the next two pages is a sampling of environmental groups, including many major ones and some lesser-known organizations. You can learn more by writing to them for information. After this list of citizen groups is a list of agencies of the United States government. The most comprehensive listing of all such groups and agencies in the U.S. and Canada is the *Conservation Directory,* published annually by the National Wildlife Federation. The NWF's address is on the following page.

African Wildlife Foundation
1717 Massachusetts Avenue NW
Washington, DC 20036

American Rivers
801 Pennsylvania Avenue NW
Washington, DC 20003

Bat Conservation International
P.O. Box 162603
Austin, TX 78716

The Cousteau Society
870 Greenbrier Circle, Suite 402
Chesapeake, VA 23320

Defenders of Wildlife
1101 Fourteenth Street NW
Suite 1400
Washington, DC 20005

Earth Island Institute
300 Broadway, Suite 28
San Francisco, CA 94133

Environmental Defense Fund
257 Park Avenue South
New York, NY 10010

Friends of the Earth
1025 Vermont Avenue NW
Suite 300
Washington, DC 20005

Greenpeace
1436 U Street NW
Washington, DC 20009

Izaak Walton League of America
707 Conservation Lane
Gaithersburg, MD 20878

National Audubon Society
700 Broadway
New York, NY 10003

National Parks and Conservation
Association
1776 Massachusetts Avenue NW
Washington, DC 20036

National Wildlife Federation
1400 Sixteenth Street NW
Washington, DC 20036

Natural Resources Defense Council
40 West Twentieth Street
New York, NY 10011

The Nature Conservancy
1815 North Lynn Street
Arlington, VA 22209

North American Bluebird Society
P.O. Box 6295
Silver Spring, MD 20906

Rainforest Action Network
450 Sansome Street, Suite 700
San Francisco, CA 94111

Save the Manatee Club
500 North Maitland Avenue
Maitland, FL 32751

Sea Shepherd Conservation Society
P.O. Box 628
Venice, CA 90294

Scenic Hudson, Inc.
9 Vassar Street
Poughkeepsie, NY 12601
(formerly the Scenic Hudson
Preservation Conference)

Sierra Club
730 Polk Street
San Francisco, CA 94109

Student Conservation Association
P.O. Box 550
Charlestown, NH 03603

The Wilderness Society
900 Seventeenth Street NW
Washington, DC 20006

World Wildlife Fund
1250 Twenty-fourth Street NW
Washington, DC 20037

Worldwatch Institute
1776 Massachusetts Avenue NW
Washington, DC 20036

Zero Population Growth
1400 Sixteenth Street NW
Suite 320
Washington, DC 20036

# Government Agencies

In addition to these agencies of the U.S. government, every state capital is home to at least one agency, often called the Department of Natural Resources, that is responsible for dealing with many environmental problems.

Department of Agriculture
14th Street and Independence Avenue
Washington, DC 20250
Within this department are the Soil Conservation Service (P.O. Box 2890, Washington, DC 20013) and the Forest Service (P.O. Box 96090, Washington, DC 20090), which is responsible for managing the national forests.

Department of Energy
1000 Independence Avenue SW
Washington, DC 20585

Department of the Interior
1849 C Street NW
Washington, DC 20240
Within this department are the Bureau of Land Management (same address), which administers almost half of all federally owned lands; Fish and Wildlife Service (same address), which has many responsibilities, including managing federal wildlife refuges; National Park Service, P.O. Box 37127, Washington, DC 20013.

Environmental Protection Agency
401 M Street SW
Washington, DC 20460

# Further Reading

The following books and articles cover a broad range of environmental literature. Most are recently published, but the references also include decades-old classics (mentioned in the text) that played key roles in environmental thoughts and actions.

Abbey, Edward. *Desert Solitaire.* New York: McGraw-Hill, 1968.

———. *The Monkey Wrench Gang.* New York: Avon Books, 1976.

Abramovitz, Janet. "Putting a Value on Nature's 'Free' Services." *World Watch* (January–February 1998), pp. 10–19.

Anonymous. *Acid Rain: A Continuing National Tragedy.* Elizabethtown, NY: The Adirondack Council, 1998.

Baskin, Yvonne, ed. *The Work of Nature: How the Diversity of Life Sustains Us.* Washington, DC: Island Press, 1997.

Bolling, David. *How to Save a River: A Handbook for Citizen Action.* Washington, DC: Island Press, 1994.

Bormann, F. Herbert, and Stephen R. Kellert, eds. *Ecology, Economics, and Ethics: The Broken Circle.* New Haven, CT: Yale University Press, 1994.

Brown, Lester, et al. *Saving the Planet: How to Shape an Environmentally Sustainable Global Economy.* New York: W. W. Norton, 1991.

Carson, Rachel. *Silent Spring,* 25th anniversary ed. Boston: Houghton Mifflin, 1987.

Culotta, Elizabeth. "Bringing Back the Everglades." *Science* (June 23, 1995), pp. 1688–90.

Daily, Gretchen, ed. *Nature's Services: Societal Dependence on Natural Ecosystems.* Washington, DC: Island Press, 1997.

Earthworks Group. *50 Simple Things You Can Do to Save the Earth.* Berkeley, CA: The Earthworks Press, 1990.

Ehrlich, Paul, and Anne Ehrlich. *Betrayal of Science and Reason: How Anti-Environmental Rhetoric Threatens Our Future.* Washington, DC: Island Press, 1996.

Frome, Michael. *Conscience of a Conservationist.* Knoxville: University of Tennessee Press, 1989.

Gelbspan, Ross. *The Heat Is On: The High-Stakes Battle over Earth's Threatened Climate.* New York: Addison Wesley, 1997.

Gore, Al. *Earth in the Balance: Ecology and the Human Spirit.* Boston: Houghton Mifflin, 1992.

Helvarg, David. "The Big Green Spin Machine: Corporations and Environmental PR." *Amicus Journal* (Summer 1996), pp. 13–21.

Lear, Linda. *Rachel Carson: Witness for Nature.* New York: Henry Holt, 1997.

Leopold, Aldo. *A Sand County Almanac.* New York: Oxford University Press, 1964.

Lubchenco, Jane. "Entering the Century of the Environment: A New Social Contract for Science." *Science* (January 23, 1998), pp. 491–97.

McKibben, Bill. *The End of Nature.* New York: Random House, 1989.

———. "What Good Is a Forest?" *Audubon* (May–June 1996), pp. 54–63.

Myers, Norman, and Julian Simon. *Scarcity or Abundance: A Debate on the Environment.* New York: W. W. Norton, 1994.

O'Meara, Molly. "The Risks of Disrupting Climate." *World Watch* (November–December 1997), pp. 10–24.

Pinchot, Gifford. *The Fight for Conservation.* Seattle: University of Washington Press, 1967.

Pringle, Laurence. *Living Treasure: Saving Earth's Threatened Biodiversity.* New York: Morrow Junior Books, 1991.

———. *Oil Spills.* New York: Morrow Junior Books, 1993.

———. *Rain of Troubles: The Science and Politics of Acid Rain.* New York: Macmillan, 1988.

———. *Restoring Our Earth.* Springfield, NJ: Enslow Publishers, 1987.

———. *Taking Care of the Earth: Kids in Action,* Honesdale, PA: Boyds Mills Press, 1996.

———. *Vanishing Ozone: Protecting Earth from Ultraviolet Radiation.* New York: Morrow Junior Books, 1995.

Renner, Michael. "Saving the Earth, Creating Jobs." *World Watch* (January–February 1992), pp. 10–17.

Rolston, Holmes. *Environmental Ethics: Duties to and Values in the Natural World.* Philadelphia: Temple University Press, 1988.

Safina, Carl. *Song for the Blue Ocean: Encounters along the World's Coasts and beneath the Seas.* New York: Henry Holt, 1998.

Scheffer, Victor. *The Shaping of Environmentalism in America.* Seattle: University of Washington Press, 1991.

Schumacher, E. F. *Small Is Beautiful.* New York: Perennial Library/Harper & Row, 1975.

Selcraig, Bruce. "Reading, 'Riting, and Ravaging: The Three Rs, Brought to You by Corporate America and the Far Right." *Sierra* (May–June 1998), pp. 60–65, 86, 89–92.

Shabecoff, Philip. *A Fierce Green Fire: The American Environmental Movement.* New York: Hill and Wang, 1993.

Schmidt, Karen. "Green Education under Fire." *Science* (December 13, 1996), pp. 1828–30.

Snow, Donald, ed. *Voices from the Environmental Movement: Perspectives for a New Era.* Washington, DC: Island Press, 1992.

Stefoff, Rebecca. *The American Environmental Movement.* New York: Facts on File, 1995.

Stegner, Wallace. "It All Began with Conservation." *Smithsonian* (April 1990), pp. 35–40.

Thoreau, Henry David. *Walden; or, Life in the Woods.* New York: Random House, 1992.

Udall, Stewart. *The Quiet Crisis.* New York: Holt, Rinehart and Winston, 1963.

Wargo, John. *Our Children's Toxic Legacy: How Science and Law Fail to Protect Us from Pesticides.* New Haven, CT: Yale University Press, 1996.

Weber, Peter. "A Place for Pesticides?" *World Watch* (May–June 1992), pp. 18–25.

Williams, Ted. "Natural Allies." *Sierra* (September–October 1996), pp. 46–53, 69.

———. "Silent Scourge." *Audubon* (January–February 1997), pp. 28–35.

Wilson, Edward O. *The Diversity of Life.* Cambridge, MA: Belknap Press of Harvard University Press, 1992.

# Index

*Illustrations are indicated by italic page numbers.*